ENVIRONMENTAL REMEDIATION TECHNOLOGIES, REGULATIONS AND SAFETY

FEDERAL MANAGEMENT OF WILDLAND FIRE

KEY CHANGES AND PERSPECTIVES ON POLICY

ENVIRONMENTAL REMEDIATION TECHNOLOGIES, REGULATIONS AND SAFETY

Additional books in this series can be found on Nova's website under the Series tab.

Additional e-books in this series can be found on Nova's website under the eBooks tab.

ENVIRONMENTAL REMEDIATION TECHNOLOGIES, REGULATIONS AND SAFETY

FEDERAL MANAGEMENT OF WILDLAND FIRE

KEY CHANGES AND PERSPECTIVES ON POLICY

REBECCA SALAZAR
EDITOR

nova publishers
New York

Library of Congress Cataloging-in-Publication Data

ISBN: 978-1-63484-864-0

Published by Nova Science Publishers, Inc. † New York

CONTENTS

PREFACE

Wildland fire plays an important ecological role in maintaining healthy ecosystems. Over the past century, however, various land management practices, including fire suppression, have disrupted the normal frequency of fires and have contributed to larger and more severe wildland fires. Wildland fires cost billions to fight each year, result in loss of life, and cause damage to homes and infrastructure. This book examines key changes the federal wildland fire agencies have made in their approach to wildland fire management since 2009; how the agencies assess the effectiveness of their wildland fire management programs; and how the agencies determine the distribution of their wildland fire management resources.

In: Federal Management of Wildland Fire
Editor: Rebecca Salazar
ISBN: 978-1-63484-864-0

Chapter 1

WILDLAND FIRE MANAGEMENT: AGENCIES HAVE MADE SEVERAL KEY CHANGES BUT COULD BENEFIT FROM MORE INFORMATION ABOUT EFFECTIVENESS*

United States Government Accountability Office

WHY GAO DID THIS STUDY

Wildland fire plays an important ecological role in maintaining healthy ecosystems. Over the past century, however, various land management practices, including fire suppression, have disrupted the normal frequency of fires and have contributed to larger and more severe wildland fires. Wildland fires cost billions to fight each year, result in loss of life, and cause damage to homes and infrastructure. In fiscal years 2009 through 2014, the five federal wildland fire agencies obligated a total of $8.3 billion to suppress wildland fires.

GAO was asked to review multiple aspects of federal wildland fire management across the five federal wildland fire management agencies. This report examines (1) key changes the federal wildland fire agencies have made

* This is an edited, reformatted and augmented version of the United States Government Accountability Office publication, GAO-15-772, dated September 2015.

in their approach to wildland fire management since 2009, (2) how the agencies assess the effectiveness of their wildland fire management programs, and (3) how the agencies determine the distribution of their wildland fire management resources. GAO reviewed laws, policies, and guidance related to wildland fire management; reviewed agency performance measures; analyzed obligation data for fiscal years 2004 through 2014; and interviewed officials from the five agencies, as well as Interior's Office of Wildland Fire.

WHAT GAO RECOMMENDS

GAO recommends that the agencies develop specific criteria for selecting wildland fires for review and conducting the reviews, and revise agency policies accordingly. The agencies generally agreed with GAO's findings and recommendations.

WHAT GAO FOUND

Since 2009, the five federal agencies responsible for wildland fire management— the Forest Service within the Department of Agriculture and the Bureau of Indian Affairs, Bureau of Land Management, Fish and Wildlife Service, and National Park Service in the Department of the Interior—have made several key changes in their approach to wildland fire management. One key change was the issuance of agency guidance in 2009 that provided managers with more flexibility in responding to wildland fires. This change allowed managers to consider different options for response given land management objectives and the risk posed by the fire. The agencies also worked with nonfederal partners to develop a strategy aimed at coordinating wildland fire management activities around common goals. The extent to which the agencies' steps have resulted in on-the- ground changes varied across agencies and regions, however, and officials identified factors, such as proximity to populated areas, that may limit their implementation of some changes.

The agencies assess the effectiveness of their wildland fire management programs in several ways, including through performance measures and reviews of specific wildland fires. The agencies are developing new performance measures, in part to help better assess the results of their current emphasis on risk-based management, according to agency officials. However, the agencies have not consistently followed agency policy regarding fire reviews, which calls for reviews of all fires resulting in federal suppression expenditures of $10 million or more, nor have they used specific criteria for the reviews they have conducted. GAO has previously found that it is important for agencies to collect performance information to inform key management decisions and to identify problems and take corrective actions. Forest Service and Interior officials said focusing only on suppression costs does not allow them to identify the most useful fires for review, and they told GAO they are working to improve their criteria for selecting fires to review and conducting these reviews. Forest Service officials did not indicate a time frame for their efforts, and while they provided a draft update of their policy manual, it did not contain specific criteria. Interior officials told GAO they expect to develop criteria by the end of 2015, but did not provide information about how they planned to develop such criteria or the factors they would consider. By developing specific criteria for selecting fires to review and conducting reviews, and making commensurate changes to agency policies, the agencies may enhance their ability to help ensure that their fire reviews provide useful information about the effectiveness of their wildland fire activities.

The Forest Service and Interior determine the distribution of fire management resources for three primary wildland fire activities of suppression, preparedness, and fuel reduction in part on the basis of historical funding amounts. For suppression, the Forest Service and Interior manage suppression funding as needed for responding to wildland fires, estimating required resources using the average of the previous 10 years of suppression obligations. For preparedness and fuel reduction, the Forest Service and Interior distribute resources based primarily on historical amounts. Both are working to distribute resources in ways that better reflect current conditions, including developing new systems that they stated they plan to begin using in fiscal year 2016.

ABBREVIATIONS

BIA	Bureau of Indian Affairs
BLM	Bureau of Land Management
FLAME	Federal Land Assistance, Management, and Enhancement Act of 2009

FWS	Fish and Wildlife Service
HFPAS	Hazardous Fuels Prioritization and Allocation System
NFMAS	National Fire Management Analysis System
NPS	National Park Service
WFDSS	Wildland Fire Decision Support System
WUI	wildland-urban interface

* * *

September 16, 2015

The Honorable Raúl Grijalva
Ranking Member
Committee on Natural Resources
House of Representatives

The Honorable Alan Lowenthal
Ranking Member
Subcommittee on Energy and Mineral Resources
Committee on Natural Resources
House of Representatives

The Honorable Peter DeFazio
House of Representatives

Wildland fire plays an important ecological role in maintaining healthy ecosystems, with many ecosystems being adapted to or dependent upon fire. However, over the past century, various land management practices, including fire suppression, have disrupted the normal frequency of fires in many forest and rangeland ecosystems across the United States, resulting in abnormally dense accumulations of vegetation. According to scientific reports, this altered landscape, combined with drought and other climate stressors, has contributed to larger and more severe wildland fires, and many scientists and researchers expect fires to become even larger and more severe in the future.[1] In addition, continued development occurring in and around wildlands, an area often called the wildland-urban interface (WUI), has placed more people, businesses, and other valuable infrastructure at risk from wildland fire. Wildland fires cost billions of dollars every year and have resulted in loss of life, both of residents as well as firefighters, and damage to homes and infrastructure. Wildland fires have also destroyed or damaged important cultural resources and critical natural resources, such as watersheds that provide drinking water to communities.

Five federal agencies—the Forest Service within the Department of Agriculture and the Bureau of Indian Affairs (BIA), Bureau of Land Management (BLM), Fish and Wildlife Service (FWS), and National Park Service (NPS) within the Department of the Interior—are responsible for managing wildland fires on federal lands. State forestry agencies and other entities—including tribal, county, city, and rural fire departments— have primary responsibility for managing wildland fires on nonfederal lands and share responsibility for protecting homes and other private structures.

As noted in the *2014 Quadrennial Fire Review*, an interagency report prepared for the federal wildland fire agencies, balancing the need to suppress unwanted wildland fires to protect people and resources with the need to recognize fire's natural role on the landscape is a complex task.[2] In recent decades, increased wildland fire intensity has placed greater demands on federal wildland fire management programs and prompted new policies and efforts aimed at implementing more effective management strategies to manage wildland fire. These efforts take on greater importance in light of constrained budgets and the amount spent by federal agencies on wildland fire management; in fiscal years 2009 through 2014, for example, federal agencies reported obligating a total of $8.3 billion to suppress wildland fires. According to several agency reports, given the current condition of the nation's landscapes and the future outlook for wildland fires, increasing demands on federal wildland fire management programs are likely to persist.[3]

The five agencies' wildland fire management efforts have undergone multiple reviews, including by us and the Offices of Inspector General for Agriculture and Interior, to assess whether federal wildland fire activities and policies are appropriate and are being carried out in a cost-effective manner. We last conducted a comprehensive review of federal wildland fire management in 2009.[4] The resulting report provided an overview of the agencies' efforts to address wildland fire issues, including the progress the agencies had made in managing wildland fire.

You asked us to review multiple aspects of federal wildland fire management across the five federal land management agencies responsible for wildland fire management. This report examines (1) key changes the federal wildland fire agencies have made in their approach to wildland fire management since 2009, (2) how the agencies assess the effectiveness of their wildland fire management programs, and (3) how the agencies determine the distribution of their wildland fire management resources.

To perform this work, we reviewed laws, policies, and guidance related to federal wildland fire management. We also interviewed headquarters officials from each of the five federal land management agencies responsible for wildland fire management (the Forest Service, BIA, BLM, FWS, and NPS), as well as Interior's Office of Wildland Fire.[5] We also conducted interviews of officials from each of the 9 Forest Service regional offices and 11 of BLM's 12 state offices,[6] as well as from selected BIA, FWS, and NPS regions.[7] We focused these regional interviews primarily on the Forest Service and BLM because those agencies receive the greatest percentage of federal wildland fire funding. For BIA, FWS, and NPS, we selected the two regions from each agency that received the most funds—BIA's Northwest and Western Regions, FWS's Southwest and Southeast Regions, and NPS's Pacific West and Intermountain Regions. During these interviews, we asked about changes to the agencies' approach to wildland fire management, agency efforts to assess the effectiveness of their wildland fire management activities, and agency processes for determining the distribution of fire management resources.

To address our first objective, we reviewed agency documents, including policies, guidance, and reports such as the *Quadrennial Fire Review*, to identify changes the agencies have made to their approach to managing wildland fire since 2009, efforts the agencies have undertaken to address wildland fire management challenges, and any agency-identified improvements resulting from those changes. To further our understanding of these issues, we interviewed agency headquarters and regional officials about these changes. In particular, we asked about the extent to which changes to the agencies' wildland fire management approaches have occurred or are planned and how the regions implemented national direction and policy. We analyzed the responses provided to us during the interviews to identify prominent changes since 2009 and challenges associated with implementing them.

To address our second objective, we reviewed documents, such as agency strategic plans and budget justifications, and interviewed officials to identify key performance measures and other mechanisms the agencies use to determine the effectiveness of their wildland fire management programs, as well as any changes they are making in this area. We also reviewed legislative and agency direction related to fire reviews, including agency policies and the *Interagency Standards for Fire and Fire Aviation Operations*, and we reviewed reports resulting from fire reviews conducted by the agencies since 2009. We compared agency practices for conducting fire reviews to direction contained in relevant agency policy. To obtain additional insight into the use of performance information on the part of federal agencies, we also reviewed our previous reports related to agencies' use of performance information.

To address our third objective, we reviewed relevant agency budget documentation, including annual budget justifications, as well as information about the tools and systems the agencies use to distribute funds and resources, to identify the agencies' distribution processes. We did not assess the design or the use of these tools or systems. We interviewed agency officials about their agencies' processes for budget formulation and resource distribution, including any differences among agencies or regional offices in how funds and resources are distributed, as well as the extent to which distribution decisions have changed in recent years at the headquarters and regional levels for each of the five agencies. We also obtained and analyzed Forest Service and Interior data on wildland fire management obligations for fiscal years 2004 through 2014, analyzing the data in both nominal (actual) and constant (adjusted for inflation) terms. We reviewed budget documents and obligation data provided by the agencies and interviewed agency officials knowledgeable about the data, and we found the data to be sufficiently reliable for the purposes of this report. Unless otherwise noted, dollar figures provided in this report represent obligations reported to us by the agencies and are presented in nominal dollars, unadjusted for inflation.[8] Appendix I describes our objectives, scope, and methodology in more detail.

We conducted this performance audit from August 2014 to September 2015 in accordance with generally accepted government auditing standards. Those standards require that we plan and perform the audit to obtain sufficient, appropriate evidence to provide a reasonable basis for our findings and conclusions based on our audit objectives. We believe that the evidence obtained provides a reasonable basis for our findings and conclusions based on our audit objectives.

BACKGROUND

Wildland fires are both natural and inevitable and play an important ecological role on the nation's landscapes. These fires have long shaped the composition of forests and grasslands, periodically reduced vegetation densities, and stimulated seedling regeneration and growth in some species. Wildland fires can be ignited by lightning or by humans either accidentally or intentionally. As we have described in previous reports, however, various land use and management practices over the past century—including fire suppression, grazing, and timber harvesting—have reduced the normal frequency of fires in many forest and rangeland ecosystems.[9] These practices contributed to abnormally dense, continuous accumulations of vegetation, which in turn can fuel uncharacteristically severe wildland fires in certain ecosystems.

According to scientific reports, several other factors have contributed to overall changes to ecosystems and the landscapes on which they depend, altering natural fire regimes and contributing to an increased frequency or intensity of wildland fire in some areas. For example, the introduction and spread of highly flammable invasive nonnative grasses, such as cheatgrass, along with the expanded range of certain flammable native species, such as western juniper, in the Great Basin region of the western United States—including portions of California, Idaho, Nevada, Oregon, and Utah— have increased the frequency and intensity of fire in the sagebrush steppe ecosystem.[10] Changing climate conditions, including drier conditions in certain parts of the country, have increased the length and severity of wildfire seasons, according to many scientists and researchers.[11] For example, in the western United States, the average number of days in the fire season has increased from approximately 200 in 1980 to approximately 300 in 2013, according to the *2014 Quadrennial Fire Review.*[12] In Texas and Oklahoma this increase was even greater, with the average fire season increasing from fewer than 100 days to more than 300 during this time. According to the U.S. Global Change Research Program's 2014 National Climate Assessment, projected climate changes suggest that western forests in the United States will be increasingly affected by large and intense fires that occur more frequently.[13] Figure 1 shows the wildfire hazard potential across the country as of 2014.

In addition, development in the wildland-urban interface (WUI) has continued to increase over the last several decades, increasing wildland fire's risk to life and property. According to the *2014 Quadrennial Fire Review*, 60 percent of new homes built in the United States since 1990 were built in the WUI, and the WUI includes 46 million single-family homes and an estimated population of more than 120 million. In addition to increased residential development, other types of infrastructure are located in the WUI, including power lines, campgrounds and other recreational facilities, communication towers, oil and gas wells, and roads. Some states, such as New Mexico and Wyoming, have experienced significant increases in oil and gas development over the past decade, adding to the infrastructure agencies may need to protect.

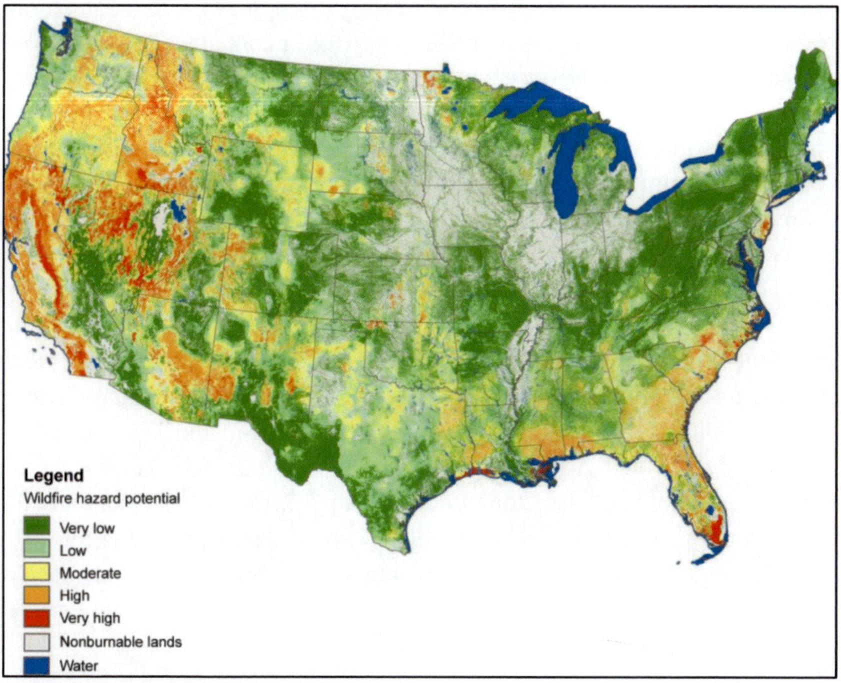

Source: Forest Service. |GAO-15-772

Note: According to the Forest Service, areas mapped with higher values of wildfire hazard potential represent fuels with a higher probability of extreme fire behavior under conducive weather conditions. The map does not represent a forecast or fire outlook for any particular season.

Figure 1. Wildfire Hazard Potential for the Contiguous 48 States, 2014.

Primary Federal Land Management Agencies with Wildland Fire Management Responsibilities

Under the National Forest Management Act and the Federal Land Policy and Management Act of 1976, respectively, the Forest Service and BLM manage their lands for multiple uses such as protection of fish and wildlife habitat, forage for livestock, recreation, timber harvesting, and energy production.[14] FWS and NPS manage federal lands under legislation that primarily calls for conservation; management for activities such as harvesting timber for commercial use is generally precluded.[15] BIA is responsible for the administration and management of lands held in trust by the United States for Indian tribes, individuals, and Alaska Natives. These five agencies manage about 700 million surface acres of land in the United States, including national forests and grasslands, national wildlife refuges, national parks, and Indian reservations. The Forest Service and BLM manage the majority of these lands. The Forest Service manages about 190 million acres, BLM manages about 250 million acres; and BIA, FWS, and NPS manage 55, 89, and 80 million acres, respectively. Figure 2 shows the lands managed by each of these five agencies.

Severe wildland fires and the vegetation that fuels them may cross the administrative boundaries of the individual federal land management agencies or the boundaries between federal and nonfederal lands. State forestry agencies and other entities—including tribal, county, city, and rural fire departments—share responsibility for protecting homes and other private structures and have primary responsibility for managing wildland fires on nonfederal lands. Most of the increased development in the WUI occurs on nonfederal lands, and approximately 70,000 communities nationwide are considered to be at high risk from wildland fire.[16] Some of these communities have attempted to reduce risk of wildland fire through programs aimed at improving fire risk awareness and promoting steps to reduce their risk, such as the Firewise Communities program.[17]

Key Components of Wildland Fire Management

Wildland fire management consists of three primary components: preparedness, suppression, and fuel reduction.[18]

- **Preparedness.** To prepare for a wildland fire season, the five land management agencies acquire firefighting assets—including firefighters, fire engines, aircraft, and other equipment—and station them either at individual federal land management units or at centralized dispatch locations in advance of expected wildland fire activity. The primary purpose of acquiring these assets is to respond to fires before they become large—a response referred to as initial attack. The agencies fund the assets used for initial attack primarily from their wildland fire preparedness accounts.
- **Suppression.** When a fire starts, interagency policy calls for the agencies to consider land management objectives—identified in land and fire management plans developed by each land management

unit—and the structures and resources at risk when determining whether or how to suppress the fire. A wide spectrum of strategies is available to choose from, and the land manager at the affected local unit is responsible for determining which strategy to use—from conducting all-out suppression efforts to monitoring fires within predetermined areas in order to provide natural resource benefits. When a fire is reported, the agencies are to follow a principle of closest available resource, meaning that, regardless of jurisdiction, the closest available firefighting equipment and personnel respond. In instances when fires escape initial attack and grow large, the agencies respond using an interagency system that mobilizes additional firefighting assets from federal, state, and local agencies, as well as private contractors, regardless of which agency or agencies have jurisdiction over the burning lands. The agencies use an incident management system under which specialized teams are mobilized to respond to wildland fires, with the size and composition of the team determined by the complexity of the fire. Federal agencies typically fund the costs of these activities from their wildland fire suppression accounts.

- **Fuel reduction.** Fuel reduction refers to agencies' efforts to reduce potentially hazardous vegetation that can fuel fires, such as brush and "ladder fuels" (i.e., small trees and other vegetation that can carry fire vertically to taller vegetation such as large trees), in an effort to reduce the potential for severe wildland fires, lessen the damage caused by fires, limit the spread of flammable invasive species, and restore and maintain healthy ecosystems.[19] The agencies use multiple approaches for reducing this vegetation, including setting fires under controlled conditions (prescribed burns), mechanical thinning, herbicides, certain grazing methods, or combinations of these and other approaches. The agencies typically fund these activities from their fuel reduction accounts.

Risk is an inherent element of wildland fire management. Federal agencies acknowledge this risk, and agency policies emphasize the importance of managing their programs accordingly. For example, Forest Service guidance states that "the wildland fire management environment is complex and possesses inherent hazards that can—even with reasonable mitigation—result in harm." According to a 2013 Forest Service report on decision making for wildfires, risk management is to be applied at all levels of wildfire decision making, from the individual firefighter on the ground facing changing environmental conditions to national leaders of the fire management agencies weighing limited budgets against increasingly active fire seasons.[20] For example, the report explains that, during individual wildland fires, risk can be defined as "a function of values, hazards, and probability."[21]

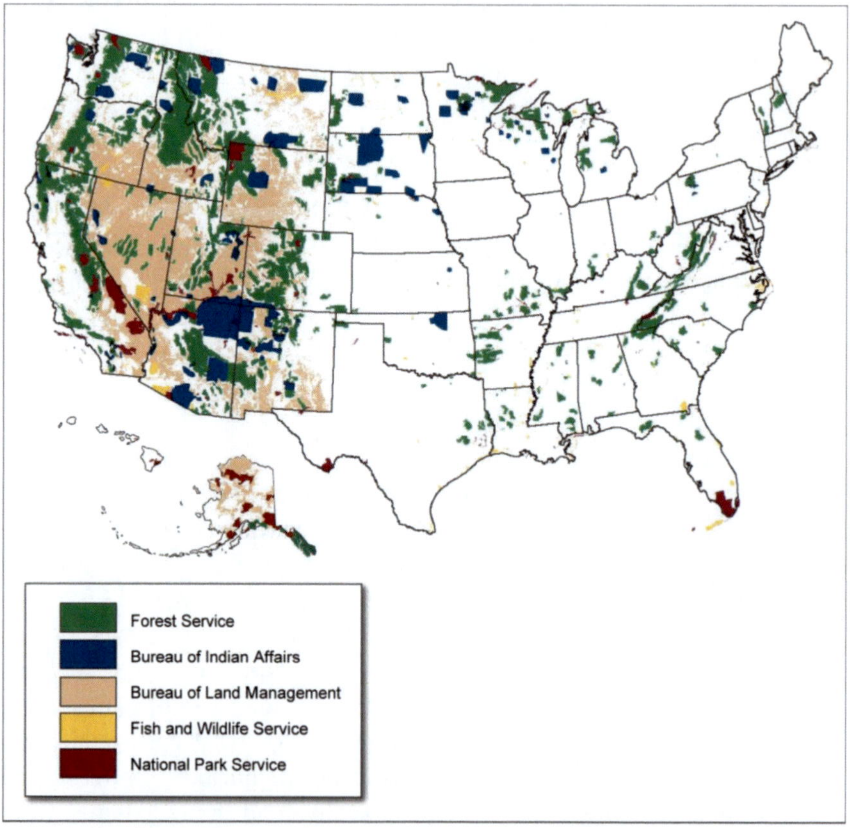

Sources: GAO analysis of U. S. Geological Survey's National Atlas website data; Map Resources (map). |GAO-15-772

Figure 2. Lands Managed by the Five Federal Land Management Agencies Responsible for Wildland Fire Management.

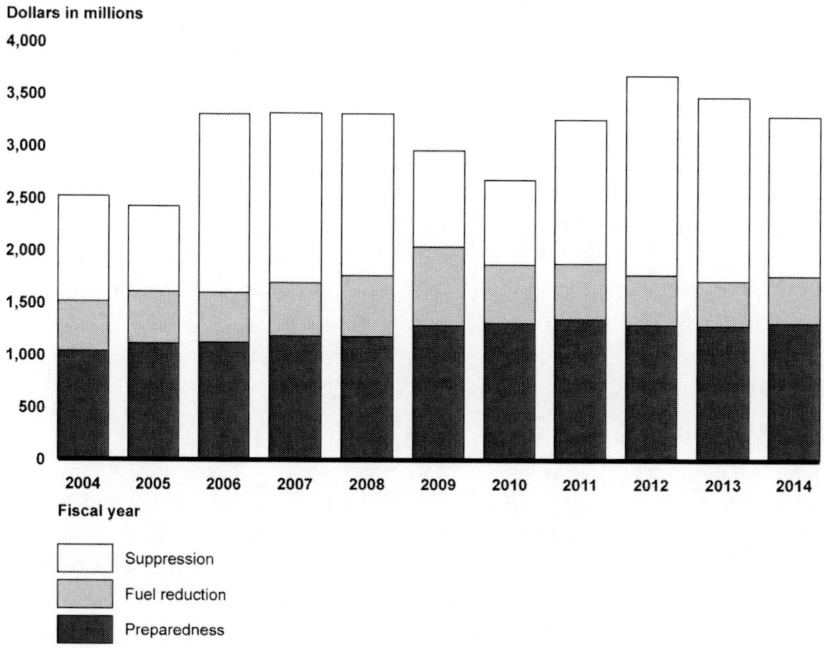

Source: GAO analysis of Forest Service and Interior data. |GAO-15-772

Figure 3. Obligations for Suppression, Fuel Reduction, and Preparedness, Forest Service and Department of the Interior, Fiscal Years 2004 through 2014.

Funding for Federal Wildland Fire Management

Congress, the Office of Management and Budget, federal agency officials, and others have raised questions about the growing cost of federal wildland fire management. According to a 2015 report by Forest Service researchers, for example, the amount the Forest Service spends on wildland fire management has increased from 17 percent of the agency's total funds in 1995 to 51 percent of funds in 2014.[22] The report noted that this has come at the cost of other land management programs within the agency, such as vegetation and watershed management, some of which support activities intended to reduce future wildfire damage. From fiscal years 2004 through 2014, the Forest Service and Interior agencies obligated $14.9 billion for suppression, $13.4 billion for preparedness, and $5.7 billion for fuel reduction. Figure 3 shows the agencies' total obligations for these three components of wildland fire management for fiscal years 2004 through 2014.

After receiving its annual appropriation, the Forest Service allocates preparedness and fuel reduction funds to its nine regional offices, and those offices in turn allocate funds to individual field units (national forests and grasslands). Interior's Office of Wildland Fire, upon receiving its annual appropriation, allocates preparedness and fuel reduction funds to BIA, BLM, FWS, and NPS. These agencies then allocate funds to their regional or state offices, which in turn allocate funds to individual field units (e.g. national parks or national wildlife refuges). The Forest Service and Interior agencies do not allocate suppression funding to their regions. These funds are managed at the national level.

Federal Wildland Fire Policy History

Federal wildland fire management policy has evolved over the past century in response to changing landscape conditions and greater recognition of fire's role in maintaining resilient and healthy ecosystems. According to wildland fire historians, in the late 1800s and early 1900s, the nation experienced a series of large and devastating fires that burned millions of acres, including highly valued timber stands. In May 1908, federal legislation authorized the Forest Service to use any of its appropriations to fight fires.[23] During the following decades, the Forest Service and Interior agencies generally took the view that fires were damaging and should be suppressed quickly, with policies and practices evolving gradually. For example, in 1935, the Forest Service issued the "10 a.m. policy," which stated that whenever possible, every fire should be contained by 10 a.m. on the day after it was reported. In more remote areas, suppression policies had minimal effect until fire towers, lookout systems, and roads in the 1930s facilitated fire detection and fire deployment.[24] The use of aircraft to drop fire retardants—that is, chemicals designed to slow fire growth—began in the 1950s, according to agency documents. Subsequent to the introduction of the 10 a.m. policy, some changes to agency policies lessened the emphasis on suppressing all fires, as some federal land managers took note of the unintended consequences of suppression and took steps to address those effects. In 1943, for example, the Chief of the Forest Service permitted national forests to use prescribed fire to reduce fuels on a case-by-case basis. In 1968, NPS revised its fire policy, shifting its approach from suppressing all fires to managing fire by using prescribed burning and allowing fires started by lightning to burn in an effort to accomplish approved management objectives.[25] In 1978, the Forest Service revised its policy to allow naturally ignited fires to burn in some cases, and formally abandoned the 10 a.m. policy.

Two particularly significant fire events—the Yellowstone Fires of 1988, in which approximately 1.3 million acres burned, and the South Canyon Fire of 1994, in which 14 firefighters lost their lives—led the agencies to fundamentally reassess their approach to wildland fire management and develop the Federal Wildland Fire Management Policy of 1995. Under the 1995 policy, the agencies continued to move away from their emphasis on suppressing every wildland fire, seeking instead to (1) make communities and resources less susceptible to being damaged by wildland fire and (2) respond to fires so as to protect communities and important resources at risk while considering both the cost and long-term effects of that response. The policy was reaffirmed and updated in 2001, and guidance for its implementation was issued in 2003 and 2009.

In 2000, after one of the worst wildland fire seasons in 50 years, the President asked the Secretaries of Agriculture and the Interior to submit a report on managing the impact of wildland fires on communities and the environment. The report, along with congressional approval of increased appropriations for wildland fire management for fiscal year 2001, as well as other related activities, formed the basis of what is known as the National Fire Plan. The National Fire Plan emphasized the importance of reducing the buildup of hazardous vegetation that fuels severe fires, stating that unless hazardous fuels are reduced, the number of severe wildland fires and the costs associated with suppressing them would continue to increase. In 2003, Congress passed the Healthy Forests Restoration Act, with the stated purpose of, among other things, reducing wildland fire risk to communities, municipal water supplies, and other at- risk federal land through a collaborative process of planning, setting priorities for, and implementing fuel reduction projects.

Along with the development of policies governing their responses to fire, the agencies developed a basic operational framework within which they manage wildland fire incidents. For example, to respond to wildland fires affecting both federal and nonfederal jurisdictions, firefighting entities in the United States have, since the 1970s, used an interagency incident management system. This system provides an organizational structure that expands to meet a fire's complexity and demands, and allows entities to share firefighting personnel, aircraft, and equipment. Incident commanders who manage the response to each wildland fire may order firefighting assets through a three-tiered system of local, regional, and national dispatch centers. Federal, tribal, state, and local entities and private contractors supply the firefighting personnel, aircraft, equipment, and supplies which are dispatched through these centers. The agencies continue to use this framework as part of their approach to wildland fire management.

AGENCIES HAVE MADE SEVERAL KEY CHANGES IN THEIR APPROACH TO WILDLAND FIRE MANAGEMENT SINCE 2009

Since 2009, the five federal agencies have made several changes in their approach to wildland fire management. The agencies have issued fire management guidance which, among other things, gave their managers greater flexibility in responding to wildland fires by providing for responses other than full suppression of fires. In collaboration with nonfederal partners such as tribal and state governments, they have also developed a strategy aimed at coordinating federal and nonfederal wildland fire management activities around common goals, such as managing landscapes for resilience to fire-related disturbances. In addition, Interior, and BLM in particular, have placed a greater emphasis on wildland fire management efforts in the sagebrush steppe ecosystem by issuing guidance and developing strategies aimed at improving the condition of this landscape. The agencies have also taken steps to change other aspects of wildland fire management, including changes related to improving fire management technology, line officer training, and firefighter safety. Agency officials told us the agencies are moving toward a more risk-based approach to wildland fire management. The extent to which the agencies' actions have resulted in on-the-ground changes varied across agencies and regions, however, and officials identified factors, such as proximity to populated areas, that may limit their implementation of some of these actions.

Agencies Issued Guidance that Provided Greater Flexibility in Responding to Wildland Fire

The agencies have increased their emphasis on using wildland fire to provide natural resource benefits rather than seeking to suppress all fires, in particular through issuing the *2009 Guidance for Implementation of Federal Wildland Fire Management Policy*. Compared with interagency guidance issued in 2003, the 2009 guidance provided greater flexibility to managers in responding to wildland fire to achieve natural resource benefits for forests and grasslands, such as reducing vegetation densities and stimulating regeneration and growth in some species. The 2003 guidance stated that only one "management objective" could be applied to a single wildland fire—meaning that wildland fires could either be managed to meet suppression objectives or managed for continued burning to provide natural resource benefits, but not both. The 2003 guidance also restricted a manager's ability to switch between full suppression and management for natural resource benefits, even when fire conditions changed. In contrast, under the 2009 interagency guidance, managers may manage individual fires for multiple objectives, and may change the management objectives on a fire as it spreads across the landscape. For example, managers may simultaneously attempt to suppress part of a fire that is threatening infrastructure or valuable resources while allowing other parts of the same fire to burn to achieve desired natural resource benefits.[26] According to agency documents, the 2009 guidance was intended to reduce barriers to risk- informed decision making, allowing the response to be more commensurate with the risk posed by the fire, the resources to be protected, and the agencies' land management objectives.

However, agency officials varied in their opinions about the extent to which this guidance changed their management practices, with some telling us it marked a departure from their past practices, and others telling us it did not significantly change the way they managed wildland fire. Several headquarters and regional agency officials told us the guidance improved managers' ability to address natural resource needs when managing a fire, rather than simply suppressing all fires. For example, BIA officials told us that the flexibility provided through the guidance allowed managers on the San Carlos Apache Reservation in southeastern Arizona to use a variety of management strategies to manage the 2014 Skunk Fire. According to a BIA fire ecologist, managers were able to maximize firefighter safety while fostering desirable ecological benefits, including helping to restore the historical fire regime to the area.[27] In addition, Forest Service officials from several regions, including the Rocky Mountain and Intermountain Regions, told us they have used the full range of management options in the guidance more frequently over the last 5 years, and they credited the 2009 guidance for giving them the ability to manage fires and their associated risks. For example, during the 2011 Duckett Fire on the Pike-San Isabel National Forests in Colorado, managers attempted to contain part of the fire to protect a subdivision while allowing the portion of the fire uphill from the subdivision to burn into wilderness. Officials told us that, prior to the

2009 guidance, they would likely have responded to this fire by attempting full suppression, which could have put firefighters at risk at the upper part of the fire because of the steep and rugged terrain.

In contrast, other officials told us the effect of the guidance was minimal because certain factors—including proximity to populated areas, size of the land management unit, and concerns about resources necessary to monitor fires—limit their ability to manage wildland fire incidents for anything other than suppression. For example, Forest Service officials from the Eastern Region told us that they try to use fire to provide natural resource benefits where possible, but they have fewer opportunities for doing so because of the smaller size of Forest Service land units in this region, which makes it more likely the fires will cross into nonfederal land, and their proximity to many areas of WUI. Similarly, Forest Service officials from the Pacific Southwest Region told us they are limited in using the added flexibility provided through the 2009 interagency guidance in Southern California, in part because the forests there are so close to major cities. However, in other more remote areas of California, these officials said they have managed wildland fires concurrently for one or more objectives, and objectives can change as the fire spreads across the landscape. Officials from BLM's Utah State Office also told us that their changed landscape is a limiting factor in responding to wildland fire. Specifically, cheatgrass, a nonnative, highly flammable grass, has replaced much of the native vegetation of the sagebrush steppe ecosystem that used to exist on the lands they manage in western Utah. As a result, introducing fire into this area could be detrimental rather than helpful because cheatgrass's flammability makes fires difficult to control.

Several officials also told us that managing wildland fires for objectives beyond full suppression, as provided for in the 2009 guidance, is highly dependent on circumstance. Officials told us that allowing fires to burn requires the agencies to devote assets to monitoring the fires to prevent them from escaping, which—especially for long-duration fires—can reduce the assets available to respond to other fires that may occur. For example, in 2012, in response to what it predicted to be an expensive and above-normal fire season, the Forest Service issued guidance to its regions limiting the use of any strategy other than full suppression (i.e., any strategy that involved allowing fires to burn for natural resource benefits) for the remainder of that year. The Forest Service noted that it was issuing this guidance because of concerns about committing the assets necessary to monitor long-duration fires that were allowed to burn in order to provide natural resource benefits. In 2015, during the Thunder Creek fire in North Cascades National Park, concerns about the resources needed to monitor the fire if it were allowed to burn to provide natural resource benefits led NPS managers instead to order full suppression efforts to help ensure that the resources would be available for other fires. In a press release about the fire, NPS noted that experts anticipated a very high potential for wildfire in 2015, leading to agency concerns that significant fire activity throughout the west could leave few available firefighting resources later in the season.

Agencies Made Changes Intended to Formalize Collaboration with Nonfederal Partners

Another change since 2009 was the completion in 2014 of the National Cohesive Wildland Fire Management Strategy (Cohesive Strategy), developed in collaboration with partners from multiple jurisdictions (i.e., tribal, state, and local governments, nongovernmental partners, and public stakeholders) and aimed at coordinating wildland fire management activities around common wildland fire management goals.[28] The agencies have a long history of collaboration with nonfederal partners in various aspects of wildland fire management, including mobilizing firefighting resources during wildland fire incidents and conducting fuel reduction projects across jurisdictions.[29] The Cohesive Strategy is intended to set broad, strategic, nationwide direction for such collaboration.

Specifically, the Cohesive Strategy provides a nationwide framework designed to more fully integrate fire management efforts across jurisdictions, manage risks, and protect firefighters, property, and landscapes by setting "broad, strategic, and national-level direction as a foundation for implementing actions and activities across the nation."[30] The vision of the Cohesive Strategy is "to safely and effectively extinguish fire, when needed; use fire where allowable; manage our natural resources; and as a nation, live with wildland fire." The Cohesive Strategy identified three goals: (1) landscapes across all jurisdictions are resilient to fire-related disturbances in accordance with management objectives; (2) human populations and infrastructure can withstand wildfire without loss of life or property; and (3) all jurisdictions participate in developing and implementing safe, effective, and efficient risk-based wildfire management decisions. According to a senior Forest Service official, the Wildland Fire Leadership Council is responsible for providing a national, intergovernmental platform for implementing the strategy.[31] In September 2014, an interim National Cohesive Strategy

Implementation Task Group completed an implementation framework that included potential roles, responsibilities, and membership for a "national strategic committee" that is intended to provide oversight and leadership on implementing the strategy.

Agency officials differed in the extent to which they viewed the Cohesive Strategy as having a significant effect on their wildland fire management activities. On the one hand, several headquarters and regional agency officials told us the Cohesive Strategy has improved wildland fire management. For example, Forest Service officials from the Southern Region told us the Cohesive Strategy has reinforced existing work that better enabled them to collaborate on new projects, which they told us is important because nearly 85 percent of the land base in the region is privately owned, and little could be achieved without collaboration. Forest Service officials cited one instance in which they signed a regional level agreement that will cover several state chapters of The Nature Conservancy to exchange resources for fuel reduction treatment and to promote public understanding of its benefits—an action they said was supported by the Cohesive Strategy.[32] Similarly, Forest Service officials from the Intermountain Region told us about several efforts that have been implemented across their region that they attribute to the Cohesive Strategy. For example, in 2014, the Forest Service, the state of Utah, and other stakeholders collaborated on the implementation of Utah's Catastrophic Wildfire Reduction Strategy, which aims to identify where fuel treatment across the state would be most beneficial. In contrast, many officials told us they have collaborated with partners for years and did not find the additional direction provided through the Cohesive Strategy to be much different than how they already operated. For example, several regional BLM, FWS, and NPS officials told us they have long worked with nonfederal partners on issues related to wildland fire management and that the Cohesive Strategy did not change those relationships.

However, implementation of collaborative actions stemming from the Cohesive Strategy may be limited by such factors as differences in laws and policies among federal, tribal, state, and local agencies. For example, while the 2009 federal interagency guidance provided federal managers with additional flexibility in managing a single fire for multiple purposes, laws and regulations at the state and local levels typically require full suppression of all fires, according to the *2014 Quadrennial Fire Review*.[33] For example, according to California state law, state forest officials in California are "charged with the duty of preventing and extinguishing forest fires."[34]

Increased Emphasis by Interior on the Sagebrush Steppe Ecosystem

Since 2009, Interior and BLM have placed a greater emphasis on wildland fire management, restoration, and protection related to the sagebrush steppe ecosystem—particularly with respect to habitat for the greater sage-grouse. Several changes, including urbanization and increased infrastructure built in support of various activities (e.g., roads and power lines associated with oil, gas, or renewable energy projects), have altered the sagebrush steppe ecosystem in the Great Basin region of the western United States.[35] In addition, the introduction and spread of highly flammable invasive nonnative grasses such as cheatgrass have altered this ecosystem by increasing the frequency and intensity of fire. As of July 2015, FWS was evaluating whether to list the greater sage- grouse, a species reliant on the sagebrush steppe ecosystem, as a threatened and endangered species under the Endangered Species Act.[36] FWS has noted the importance of fire and fuel management activities in reducing the threat to sage-grouse habitat.[37] Beginning in 2011, BLM issued guidance to its state offices emphasizing the importance of sage-grouse habitat in fire operations and the need for fuel reduction activities to address concerns about the habitat, more than half of which is located on BLM-managed lands. In 2014, the agency issued guidance reiterating this importance and stating that it would make changes in funding to allow field units to place greater focus on reducing fire's threats in sage-grouse habitat areas.

In January 2015, the Secretary of the Interior issued a Secretarial Order to enhance policies and strategies "for preventing and suppressing rangeland fire and for restoring sagebrush landscapes impacted by fire across the West."[38] The order established the Rangeland Fire Task Force and directed it to, among other things, complete a report on activities to be implemented ahead of the 2016 Western fire season. Under the order, the task force also was to address longer term actions to implement the policy and strategy set forth by the order. In a report issued in May 2015, *An Integrated Rangeland Fire Management Strategy*, the task force called for prepositioning firefighting assets where priority sage-grouse habitat exists, including moving assets from other parts of the country as available. The goal is to improve preparedness and suppression capability during initial stages of a wildfire to increase the chances of keeping fires small and reduce the loss of sage-grouse habitat.

The report also identified actions aimed at improving the targeting of fuel reduction activities, including identifying priority landscapes and fuel management priorities within those landscapes. These actions are to be completed by the end of September 2015 and continuously improved upon in subsequent years. According to BLM state officials, the increased emphasis on sage-grouse habitat will significantly change how they manage their fuel reduction programs. BLM officials from states that include sage-grouse habitat said they expect a large increase in fuel reduction treatment funding and increased project approvals. In contrast, BLM officials from states without this habitat told us they expect significant funding decreases, limiting their capacity to address other resource issues important for nonsagebrush ecosystems.

Agencies Made Additional Changes in other Areas of Wildland Fire Management

Since 2009, the agencies also have taken steps to change other areas of wildland fire management, including technology for wildland fire planning and response, line-officer training, and firefighter safety.

Working to Improve Technology for Wildland Fire Planning and Response

Since 2009, the agencies have applied new technologies to improve wildland fire management planning and response. Prominent among them is the Wildland Fire Decision Support System (WFDSS), a Web- based decision-support tool that assists fire managers and analysts in making strategic and tactical decisions for fire incidents. WFDSS replaced older tools, some of which had been used for more than 30 years and were not meeting current fire management needs, according to the system's website.[39] According to this site, WFDSS has several advantages over the older systems, such as enabling spatial data layering,[40] increasing use of map displays, preloading information about field units' management objectives, and allowing for use in both single and multiple fire situations. Officials from several agencies told us that using WFDSS improved their ability to manage fires by allowing information from fire management plans to be loaded into WFDSS and providing substantial real-time fire information on which to make decisions. For example, one Forest Service official told us that, at one point in a recent particularly active fire season in the Pacific Northwest Region, the system processed information on approximately 20 concurrent fires that managers could monitor in real time. As a result, they were able to make strategic and risk-informed decisions about the resource allocations needed for each fire, including decisions to let some fires burn to meet natural resource benefit objectives. According to Forest Service reviews of several fires that occurred in 2012, however, some managers said WFDSS did not provide effective decision support for firefighters because the system underestimated fire behavior or did not have current information.[41]

According to officials from several agencies, another example of updated wildland fire technology has been the replacement of traditional paper- based fire management plans with electronic geospatial-based plans. Federal wildland fire management policy directs each agency to develop a fire management plan for all areas they manage with burnable vegetation. A fire management plan, among other things, identifies fire management goals for different parts of a field unit. According to an interagency document describing geospatial-based plans, agency officials expect such plans to increase efficiency because the plans can more easily be updated to account for changes in the landscape resulting from fires, fuel reduction treatments, and other management activities. In addition, the electronic format is designed to allow plans to more easily be shared across multiple users, including personnel responding to wildland fires. Agency officials mentioned other technological improvements, such as the development of an "Enterprise Geospatial Portal" providing wildland fire data in geospatial form using a Web-based platform, although many officials also told us that additional improvements are needed in wildland fire technology overall.

In addition to specific technologies, in 2012 the Forest Service and Interior issued a report titled "Wildland Fire Information and Technology: Strategy, Governance, and Investments," representing the agencies' efforts to develop a common wildland fire information and technology vision and strategy. The agencies signed a Memorandum of Understanding later that same year intended to establish a common management approach for information and technology services. Nevertheless, the *2014 Quadrennial Fire Review* concluded that the wildland fire management community does not have an agenda for innovation and technology adoption or a list of priorities, stating that the wildland fire community "sometimes struggles to define common technology priorities and implement integrated, enterprise-level solutions" and noting that there are more than 400 information technology systems in use by the wildland fire community.[42] The report provides recommendations on actions the agencies could consider for improvement; however, because it was issued in May 2015, it is too early to determine what, if any, actions the agencies have taken. In commenting on a draft of this report, Interior stated that the agencies are completing an investment strategy for wildland fire applications and supporting infrastructure, but did not provide an expected date for its completion.

Increasing Line-Officer Training

Officials from several agencies told us that, since 2009, the agencies have increased training efforts, particularly those aimed at improving line officers' knowledge about, and response to, wildland fires. Line officers are land unit managers such as national forest supervisors, BLM district managers, and national park superintendents. During a wildland fire, staff from "incident management teams" with specific wildland firefighting and management training manage the response, and line officers associated with the land unit where the fire is occurring must approve major decisions that incident management teams make during the response.[43] Officials at BLM's Oregon/Washington State Office, for example, told us they provide line officers with day-long simulation exercises, as well as shadowing opportunities that give line officers experience on actual wildland fires. Beginning in 2007, the Forest Service initiated a Line Officer Certification Program and began a coaching and mentoring program to provide on-the-ground experience for preparing line officers to act as agency administrators during wildland fires or other critical incidents. This program is aimed at providing officials that do not have wildland fire experience the opportunity to work under the advisement of a coach with wildland fire experience. According to Forest Service documents, this program has evolved substantially, in part to address the increased demand for skills necessary to manage increasingly complex wildland fires. In May 2015, the Forest Service issued guidance for the program and called for each Forest Service regional office to administer it within the regions.

Emphasizing the Primacy of Firefighter Safety

Officials told us that, since 2009, the agencies have, in some cases, changed firefighting tactics to better protect firefighters, including making greater use of natural barriers to contain fire instead of attacking fires directly. The agencies have also issued additional guidance aimed at emphasizing the primacy of firefighter safety. In 2010, the agencies developed and issued the "Dutch Creek Protocol" (named after a wildland fire where a firefighter died), which provided a standard set of protocols for wildland firefighting teams to follow during an emergency medical response or when removing and transporting personnel from a location on a fire. Both the Forest Service and

Interior have also issued agency direction stating that firefighter safety should be the priority of every fire manager.[44]

AGENCIES ASSESS EFFECTIVENESS OF THEIR PROGRAMS IN SEVERAL WAYS, BUT HAVE NOT CONSISTENTLY CONDUCTED REVIEWS THAT COULD IMPROVE RESPONSES TO WILDLAND FIRES

The agencies assess the effectiveness of their wildland fire management programs in several ways, including through performance measures, efforts to assess specific activities, and reviews of specific wildland fire incidents. Both the Forest Service and Interior are developing new performance measures and evaluations, in part to help better assess the results of their current emphasis on risk-based management, according to agency officials. In addition, the agencies have undertaken multiple efforts, such as studies, to assess the effectiveness of activities including fuel reduction treatments and aerial firefighting. The agencies also conduct reviews of their responses to wildland fires. However, they have not consistently followed agency policy in doing so or used specific criteria for selecting the fires they have reviewed, limiting their ability to help ensure that their fire reviews provide useful information and meaningful results.

Agencies Use Various Performance Measures to Assess Wildland Fire Management

Both the Forest Service and Interior use various performance measures, such as the number of WUI acres treated to reduce fuels and the percentage of wildland fires contained during initial attack, to assess their wildland fire management effectiveness. These measures are reported in, among other things, the agencies' annual congressional budget justifications. Officials from both the Forest Service and Interior told us their performance measures need improvement to more appropriately reflect their approach to wildland fire management and, in June 2015, officials from both agencies told us that they were working to improve them. For example, several performance measures for both agencies use a "stratified cost index" to help analyze suppression costs on wildfires. The index is based on a model that compares the suppression costs of fires that have similar characteristics, such as fire size, fuel types, and proximity to communities, and identifies the percentage of fires with suppression costs that exceeded the index. We found in a June 2007 report, however, that the index was not entirely reliable and that using the index as the basis for comparison may not allow the agencies to accurately identify fires where more, or more-expensive, resources than needed were used.[45] The agencies continue to use the index, but have acknowledged its shortcomings.[46] The Forest Service reported in its fiscal year 2016 budget justification to Congress that improvements were forthcoming. In April 2015, Forest Service officials told us they have incorporated detailed geospatial information into the model on which the index is based to help yield more accurate predictions of suppression expenditures and have submitted the model for peer review. Once that is complete, the agencies plan to begin to implement the updated model, but officials did not provide a time frame for doing so.

Both agencies have also made efforts to improve their performance measures to better reflect their emphasis on a risk-based approach to wildland fire management. In fiscal year 2014, Interior began using a new performance measure intended to better reflect a variety of strategies in addition to full suppression: "Percent of wildfires on DOI-managed landscapes where the initial strategy (ies) fully succeeded during the initial response phase."[47] The same year, the Forest Service began developing a performance measure intended to reflect that, in some cases, allowing naturally-ignited fires to burn can provide natural resource benefits at a lower cost and lower risk to personnel than fully suppressing the fire as quickly as possible: "Percent of acres burned by natural ignition with resource benefits." Forest Service officials told us they are working with field units to evaluate whether this measure will effectively assess their efforts to implement a risk-based approach to fire management and that they will adjust it as needed. The officials told us they plan to finalize the measure and use it in 2017.

Also, in fiscal year 2014, the Forest Service began developing a performance measure that would assess the risk that wildland fire presents to highly valued resources such as communities and watersheds. This measure is known as the "National Forest System wildfire risk index." According to the agency's fiscal year 2016 budget justification, it would create an index of relative fire risk based on the likelihood of a large fire affecting these highly valued resources. It may also incorporate factors measuring the relative importance of these resources and the expected effects that might occur from fire. The Forest Service plans to establish a national baseline measure for this index in 2015 and then periodically remeasure it, likely every 2 years, to determine if overall risk has been reduced, according to Forest Service officials. Changes that could affect the index include those resulting from fuel reduction treatments, wildland fire, forest management activities, vegetative growth, and increased WUI development, among others, according to the agency's 2016 budget justification. As with the performance measure described above, agency officials told us they will evaluate whether the measure meets their needs before adopting it; if it meets their needs, they plan to finalize the measure and use it in 2017.

Agencies Have Undertaken Multiple Efforts to Assess Effectiveness of Specific Activities

The agencies have also undertaken multiple efforts to assess the effectiveness of particular activities, such as fuel reduction and aerial firefighting. Regarding fuel reduction activities, we found in September 2007 and September 2009 that demonstrating the effectiveness of fuel reduction treatments is inherently complex and that the agencies did not have sufficient information to evaluate fuel treatment effectiveness, such as the extent to which treatments changed fire behavior.[48] Without such information, we concluded that the agencies could not ensure that fuel reduction funds were directed to the areas where they can best minimize risk to communities and natural and cultural resources. Accordingly, we recommended that the agencies take actions to develop additional information on fuel treatment effectiveness.[49] While the agencies took steps to address this recommendation, they are continuing efforts to improve their understanding of fuel treatment effectiveness. For example, the Forest Service and Interior agencies use a system called Fuel Treatment Effectiveness Monitoring to document and assess fuel reduction treatment effectiveness.[50] The Forest Service began requiring such assessments in 2011 and Interior requested such assessments be completed starting in 2012.[51] Under this approach, the agencies are to complete a monitoring report whenever a wildfire interacts with a fuel treatment and enter the information into the system. Officials told us that additional efforts are under way to help understand other aspects of fuel treatment effectiveness. For example, in February 2015, the Joint Fire Science Program completed its strategy to implement the 2014 Fuel Treatment Science Plan.[52] It includes as one of its goals the "development of measures/metrics of effectiveness that incorporate ecological, social, resilience, and resource management objectives at the regional and national level."

The Forest Service and Interior are also implementing an effort known as the Aerial Firefighting Use and Effectiveness Study, begun in 2012 to address concerns about limited performance information regarding the use of firefighting aircraft. As part of this effort, the agencies are collecting information on how aerial retardant and suppressant delivery affects fire behavior and plan to use this and other collected information to track the performance of specific aircraft types, according to the study website.[53]This will help the agencies identify ways to improve their current fleet of aircraft and inform future aerial firefighting operations and aviation strategic planning, according to the website.[54] Agency officials told us the study is not a one-time activity, but is an ongoing effort to continually provide information to help improve their use of firefighting resources.

Forest Service and Interior Agencies Have Not Consistently Conducted Reviews of Wildland Fire Incidents to Assess their Effectiveness

The Forest Service and the Interior agencies have conducted reviews to assess their effectiveness in responding to wildland fires but have not consistently followed agency policy in doing so and did not always use specific criteria for selecting the fires they have reviewed. Officials from both the Forest Service and Interior told us that current agency policy regarding fire reviews overly emphasizes the cost of wildland fire suppression rather than the effectiveness of their response to fire. However, the agencies have neither updated their policies to better reflect their emphasis on effectiveness nor established specific criteria for selecting fires for review and conducting the reviews. By developing such criteria, the agencies may enhance their ability to obtain useful, comparable information about their effectiveness in responding to wildland fires, which, in turn, may help them identify needed improvements in their wildland fire approach.

Congressional reports and agency policy have generally called for the agencies to review their responses to wildland fires involving federal expenditures of $10 million or more. For fiscal years 2003 through 2010, congressional committee reports directed the Forest Service and Interior to conduct reviews of large fire incidents, generally for the purpose of understanding how to better contain suppression costs; beginning in fiscal year

2006, these reports included a cost threshold, specifying that such reviews be conducted for fires involving federal expenditures of $10 million or more. The agencies, in turn, have each developed their own policies that generally direct them to review each fire that exceeds the $10 million threshold.[55]

The agencies, however, have not consistently conducted reviews of fire incidents meeting the $10 million threshold, in part because, according to officials, current agency policy that includes the $10 million threshold does not reflect the agencies' focus on assessing the effectiveness of their response to fire. However, the agencies have not developed specific criteria for selecting fire incidents for review. Forest Service officials told us that, rather than selecting all fires with federal expenditures of $10 million or more, they changed their approach to selecting fires to review. These officials told us that focusing exclusively on suppression costs when selecting fires limits the agency in choosing those fires where it can obtain important information and best assess management actions and ensure they are appropriate, risk-based, and effective. Forest Service officials told us the agency judgmentally selects incidents to review based on a range of broad criteria, such as complexity and national significance, taking into account political, social, natural resource, or policy concerns. Using these broad selection criteria, the Forest Service reviewed 5 wildland fires that occurred in 2012 and 10 that occurred in 2013. However, with these broad criteria it is not clear why the Forest Service selected those particular fires and not others. For example, the 2013 Rim Fire, which cost over $100 million to suppress—by far the costliest fire to suppress that year—and burned over 250,000 acres of land,[56] was not among the 2013 fires selected for review. Moreover, the reviews completed for each of those years did not use consistent or specific criteria for conducting the reviews. As of July 2015, the agency had not selected the fires it will review from the 2014 wildland fire season and, when asked, agency officials did not indicate a time frame for doing so.

Forest Service officials told us they believe it is appropriate to judgmentally select fires to provide them flexibility in identifying which fires to review and which elements of the fire response to analyze. Nevertheless, Forest Service officials also acknowledged the need to develop more specific criteria for selecting fires to review and conducting the reviews and, in July 2015, told us they are working to update their criteria for doing so. They provided us a draft update of the Forest Service policy manual, but this draft did not contain specific criteria for selecting fires for review or conducting the reviews. Moreover, officials did not provide a time frame for completing their update.

Within Interior, BLM officials told us BLM completed its last fire review based on significant cost (i.e., federal expenditures of $10 million or more) in 2013. These officials told us that BLM, similar to the Forest Service, plans to shift the emphasis of its fire reviews to evaluate management actions rather than focusing on cost, and that officials are working to determine criteria for selecting fires for review.[57] Interior headquarters officials told us that FWS and NPS have continued to follow the direction provided through their policies regarding reviews of fires that met the $10 million threshold. Interior headquarters officials, however, acknowledged the need to improve Interior's approach to selecting fires for review to focus more on information about decision making rather than fire costs. In July 2015, the officials told us they plan to develop criteria other than cost for use by all Interior agencies in selecting fires to review, and that they plan to develop standard criteria for implementing the reviews. They stated that they expect this department-wide effort to be completed by the end of calendar year 2015 but did not provide information about how they planned to develop such criteria or the factors they would consider.

Agency reports have likewise cited the need to improve both the processes for selecting fires for review and the implementation of the reviews. A 2010 report, for example, noted the importance of improving the selection of fires to review and stated that the agencies would benefit from a more productive review strategy.[58] The report said the agencies' existing approach to conducting reviews tended to produce isolated efforts and unrelated recommendations rather than establishing a consistent foundation for continuous improvement. A 2013 report assessing the usefulness of the Forest Service's five reviews of 2012 fires noted shortcomings in consistency across the reviews, including unclear criteria for selecting fires and conducting reviews, as well as limitations in the specificity of the resulting reports and recommendations.[59] As noted, both agencies have acknowledged the need to improve their criteria for selecting fires to review and conducting the reviews. By developing specific criteria in agency policies for selecting fires for review and conducting the reviews, the agencies may enhance their ability to help ensure that their fire reviews provide useful information and meaningful results. This is consistent with our previous body of work on performance management, which has shown that it is important for agencies to collect performance information to inform key management decisions, such as how to identify problems and take corrective actions and how to identify and share effective approaches.[60] By collecting such performance information, the agencies may be better positioned to identify needed improvements in their wildland fire approach and thereby use their limited resources more effectively.

Agencies Distribute Resources in Part on the Basis of Historical Amounts, but are Developing New Methods Intended to Better Reflect Current Conditions

The Forest Service and Interior determine the distribution of fire management resources in part on the basis of historical amounts but are developing new methods intended to better reflect current conditions. For suppression, the Forest Service and Interior manage funding as needed for units to respond to individual wildland fires. For preparedness, the Forest Service and Interior distribute resources based, in part on historical funding levels generated by an obsolete system.[61] The agencies are working to replace the system and develop new tools to help them distribute resources to reflect current landscape conditions, values at risk,[62] and the probability of wildland fire. For fuel reduction, until recently, the Forest Service and Interior both distributed funds using the same system. In 2014, the Forest Service began using a new system to help it distribute fuel reduction funding in ways that better reflect current conditions. Interior is working to develop a system that likewise reflects current conditions.

Agencies Fund Suppression as Needed for Responding to Wildland Fires

The agencies manage funding for suppression at the national level as needed for field units to respond to individual wildland fires. The overall amount of suppression funding the agencies obligate is determined by the complexity and number of wildland fire responses over the course of the fiscal year and can vary considerably from year to year. For example, federal agencies obligated approximately $1.7 billion for suppression in fiscal year 2006, $809 million in fiscal year 2010, and $1.9 billion in fiscal year 2012.[63] (See app. II for more detailed information about suppression obligations by the Forest Service and the Interior agencies for fiscal years 2004 through 2014.)

Each year, the agencies estimate the expected level of funding for suppression activities using the average of the previous 10 years of suppression obligations.[64] The estimated amount, however, has often been less than the agencies' actual suppression obligations, particularly for the Forest Service. In all but 2 years since 2000, Forest Service suppression obligations have exceeded the 10-year average that forms the basis of the agency's annual appropriation. To pay for wildfire suppression activities when obligations are greater than the amount appropriated for suppression, the Forest Service and Interior may transfer funds from other programs within their respective agencies as permitted by law.[65] As we found in a prior report, these transfers can affect the agencies' ability to carry out other important land management functions that are key to meeting their missions, such as restoration of forest lands and other improvements.[66] For example, according to a Forest Service report, funding transfers led to a canceled fuel reduction project on the Sante Fe National Forest and the deferral of critical habitat acquisition on the Cibola National Forest, both located in New Mexico.[67]

In their annual budget justifications for fiscal years 2015 and 2016, the agencies proposed an alternative mechanism to fund suppression activities. Under that proposal, the agencies would receive 70 percent of the standard 10-year average of suppression obligations as their appropriation for wildland fire suppression, which reflects the amount the agencies spend to suppress approximately 99 percent of wildland fires.[68]If suppression obligations exceed this amount, additional funds would be made available from a disaster funding account. Forest Service and Interior officials told us this proposal would allow them to better account for the variable nature of wildland fire seasons and reduce or eliminate the need to transfer funds from other accounts to pay for suppression. In addition, legislation pending in Congress would change how certain wildland fire suppression operations are funded.[69]

Forest Service and Interior Distribute Preparedness Funding Based in Part on an Obsolete System They Are Working to Replace

The Forest Service and Interior distribute preparedness funding to their regions and agencies, respectively, based in part on information generated from a system that is now obsolete. The agencies attempted to develop a new system to distribute preparedness funding, but ended that effort in 2014 and are now working to develop different tools and systems. In distributing preparedness funds to individual forests, some Forest Service regions have developed additional tools to help them distribute funds; similarly, three of the four Interior agencies have developed additional tools to help them distribute preparedness funds to their regions.[70] Overall preparedness obligations in 2014 totaled about $1.0 billion for the Forest Service and about $274 million for the Interior agencies.[71] (See app. II for detailed information on each of the agencies' obligations for preparedness for fiscal years 2004 through 2014.)

Forest Service and Interior Distribution of Preparedness Funds to Regions and Agencies

To determine the distribution of preparedness funds from Forest Service headquarters to its regions, and from Interior to the department's four agencies with wildland fire management responsibilities, the Forest Service and Interior rely primarily on amounts that are based on results from a budgeting system known as the National Fire Management Analysis System (NFMAS).[72] That system, however, was terminated in the early 2000s, according to agency officials. Relying on the results from the last year NFMAS was used, and making only incremental changes from year to year, the Forest Service and Interior have not made significant shifts in the funding distribution across their respective regions and agencies over time, and they have generally maintained the same number and configuration of firefighting assets (e.g., fire engines and crews) in the same geographic areas from year to year. Several agency officials, however, told us that these amounts no longer reflect current conditions, in part because of changes to the landscape resulting from increased human development, climate change, and changes to land management policies that consider natural resource values differently than they did when NFMAS was in use.

Beginning in 2002, the agencies attempted to replace NFMAS with an interagency system designed to help them determine the optimal mix and location of firefighting assets and distribute funds accordingly. In developing this system, known as the Fire Program Analysis system, the agencies' goal was to develop "a comprehensive interagency process for fire planning and budget analysis identifying cost-effective programs to achieve the full range of fire management goals and objectives."[73] According to agency documents, this effort proved problematic because of the difficulty in modeling various aspects of wildland fire management. In addition, agency officials told us it is difficult to design a system that could account for multiple agencies' different needs and varying missions. After more than a decade of work, and investment that Forest Service officials estimated at approximately $50 million, the agencies terminated the system's development in September 2014. At that time, they stated that it "only delivered inconsistent and unacceptable results."[74]

Since the termination of the Fire Program Analysis system, the agencies have continued to rely on results based on the terminated NFMAS, but have begun working on new tools to help them distribute funding and assets based on current conditions and updated information. Forest Service headquarters officials told us the agency is developing a new tool called the Wildland Fire Investment Portfolio System. According to these officials, this proposed system is intended to model scenarios such as large shifts in firefighting assets, various potential dispatch procedures, and changes in fire behavior due to climate change, which will allow managers, both at the national and individual unit level, to conduct resource trade-off analyses and assess whether assets are being used effectively. Forest Service officials told us that the agency is in the early stages of developing this proposed system and anticipates using it for planning and analysis purposes in fiscal year 2016.

Interior documents state that Interior is developing a system called the Risk-Based Wildland Fire Management model, which Interior will use to help support funding distribution decisions to the four Interior agencies for both preparedness and fuel reduction. The proposed system will assess the probability and likely intensity of wildland fire, values at risk, and the expected value of acres likely to burn. A key element of this system will be the development of strategic business plans by each of the four Interior agencies, detailing how each agency intends to distribute its preparedness and fuel reduction funding to reduce the risks from wildland fire on its lands. Interior officials said that, once the agencies provide these business plans, Interior will assess them in making funding distribution decisions among the agencies. According to several Interior agency officials, identifying priority values at risk across Interior's four agencies may be challenging given the variation in agency missions and the types of lands they manage. For example, a threatened species located primarily on BLM lands may be among BLM's highest priorities, but a forested area relied upon by an Indian tribe for its livelihood may be among BIAs' highest priorities. Interior officials told us that they expect to identify the prioritized values and issue guidance on the proposed system by the end of calendar year 2015, and then use its results to inform their fiscal year 2016 funding distributions to the four agencies.

Forest Service Regions' Distribution to Individual National Forests

Once the Forest Service distributes preparedness funding to regions, it gives regions discretion to determine how to subsequently distribute funding to individual national forests, as long as those determinations are consistent with policy and annual budget program direction. Forest Service headquarters officials told us they do not plan to direct regions to use any specific system to help inform distributions to national forests, so that regions can have flexibility in distributing their funds and take into account local conditions and priorities. According to agency officials, most regions distribute funding to individual national forests based on historical amounts resulting from NFMAS. However, two regions have changed the way they determine funding distribution to individual national forests to better reflect current landscape conditions. The Rocky Mountain Region uses a new system that ranks each of its forests according to a "risk priority score." According to regional officials, use of the system has resulted in shifts in funding across forests in the region; for example, the officials told us they have provided additional resources to forests along Colorado's Front Range because of increased development in the WUI. The Pacific Northwest Region also uses its own funding distribution tool, which considers elements such as fire occurrence and the number of available assets to develop a weighted value for each forest in the region. The region distributes the funding proportionally based on the values calculated for each forest.

Interior Agencies' Distribution to Regional Offices

Once obtaining preparedness funds from Interior, each agency—which, as noted, have their own land management responsibilities and missions—distributes these funds to its units. Three of these agencies— BLM, FWS, and NPS—use newer systems and current information, such as updated fuel characterization and fire occurrence data, to distribute funding to their regional offices. The fourth agency, BIA, generally uses historical-based amounts (i.e., NFMAS results), but has made some changes to reflect updated priorities. The regions subsequently distribute funding to individual land units, typically using the same systems. The four agencies' approaches are described below.

- **BLM.** Since 2010, BLM officials told us they have used results from the Fire Program Decision Support System to help determine funding distributions to state offices. The system analyzes BLM's fire workload and complexity using four components: fire suppression workload, fuel types, human risk, and additional fire resources, and assigns scores to state offices accordingly. Based on the resulting analyses, BLM has shifted funding across state offices to help better reflect current conditions. BLM officials told us that most states use the new system to help inform the distribution of funding to their units. BLM is also developing an additional component of the Fire Program Decision Support System to help offices determine the appropriate number of firefighting assets needed in each area. Officials expect to apply the new component with their overall system in the fall of 2015.

- **FWS.** In 2014, FWS began distributing its preparedness funding to regions using the Preparedness Allocation Tool. Officials told us that the tool uses information such as historical wildland fire occurrence, proximity to WUI areas, and other information, to inform preparedness funding distributions to regions. Agency officials told us that results from this tool did not generally identify the need for large funding shifts across units, but rather helped identify some smaller shifts to better reflect current landscape conditions. Officials with one FWS region told us that the tool has helped the agency provide better assurance that funding amounts are risk-based and transparent.
- **NPS.** Since 2013, primarily in response to their overall wildland fire management program funding reductions, NPS began using a system called the Planning Data System to determine what level of firefighting workforce the agency could afford under different budget distribution scenarios. The system generates personnel requirements for each NPS unit by establishing a minimum number of people for any unit that meets certain criteria. Those results are rolled up to also provide regional workforce requirements. The results generated from this system showed that some NPS regions, as well as individual park units, had existing wildland fire organizations that they could no longer adequately support in light of reduced budgets.[75]
- **BIA.** BIA relies primarily on historical funding amounts derived from a system similar to NFMAS. However, BIA officials told us they have made adjustments to the historical amounts using professional judgment. BIA officials told us that the regions also still primarily use historical-based amounts to distribute funding to their units. The officials told us they will wait until Interior finalizes its Risk Based Wildland Fire Management model before they develop a new funding distribution tool.

Agencies Are Working to Distribute Fuel Reduction Funding to Better Account for Current Conditions

Beginning in 2009, the Forest Service and Interior both used systems collectively known as the Hazardous Fuels Prioritization and Allocation System (HFPAS) to distribute fuel reduction funds.[76] Officials told us these systems, based on similar concepts and approaches, were developed by the agencies to provide an interagency process for distributing fuel reduction funding to the highest-priority projects.[77] Starting in 2014, the Forest Service instead began using a new system, which, according to officials, allows the agency to more effectively distribute fuel reduction funds. Interior continues to distribute fuel reduction funding to the four agencies based on funding amounts derived from HFPAS, but it plans to develop a new system for distributing funds to reflect more current conditions and risks. Overall fuel reduction obligations in 2014 totaled about $302 million for the Forest Service and about $147 million for the Interior agencies. (See app. II for detailed information on the agencies' fuel reduction obligations for fiscal years 2004 through 2014.)

Forest Service officials told us their new system identifies locations where the highest probability of wildland fire intersects with important resources, such as residential areas and watersheds critical to municipal water supplies. These officials told us the new system allows the agency to invest its fuel reduction funds in areas where there are both a high probability of wildland fires and important resources at risk. In contrast, according to officials, HFPAS in some cases prioritized funding for areas where important resources, such as extensive WUI, existed but where the potential for wildland fires was low. The new system has identified locations for funding adjustments to Forest Service regions. For example, in 2015 the agency's Eastern and Southern Regions received a smaller proportion of fuel reduction funding than they had previously received, and some western regions saw increases, because results from the system showed that the western regions had more areas with both important resources and high wildland fire potential.

The Forest Service directs its regions to distribute fuel reduction funding to national forests using methods consistent with national information, as well as with specific local data. A senior Forest Service official told us that, as a result, most regions distribute funding to individual national forests based on information generated using HFPAS, augmented with local data. One region has developed a more updated distribution approach. Specifically, in 2012, the Rocky Mountain Region, in conjunction with the Rocky Mountain Research Station and Forest Service headquarters, developed a fuel reduction funding distribution tool that generates a risk priority score for each forest in the region. The risk priority score is based on fire probability, resources at risk from fire, potential fire intensity, and historical fire occurrence. Each forest's risk priority score is used to inform the region's distribution of funding to the national forests.

Interior currently distributes fuel reduction funding to its agencies based on the funding amounts derived from HFPAS results that were last generated in 2013. Interior officials also told us they plan to stop using HFPAS results and are planning to use the new system they are developing, the Risk-Based Wildland Fire Management model, to reflect current information on conditions and risks in distributing fuel reduction funds.

Within Interior, officials from the four agencies told us they have developed, or are in the process of developing, funding distribution systems and tools while they wait for Interior to complete the Risk-Based Wildland Fire Management model. BLM, for example, uses a fuel reduction funding distribution tool that maps values at risk, including WUI, critical infrastructure, sagebrush habitat, and invasive species data. BLM combines this information with data on wildland fire probability to create a spatial illustration of the values at risk relative to potential fire occurrence. BLM then uses the results of this analysis to fund its state offices. BIA uses its own tool to distribute fuel reduction funding to its regions based on wildland fire potential data generated by the Forest Service. That information is then combined with fire occurrence history and workload capacity to generate a model that shows potential fire risk and capacity across BIA units. FWS officials told us they are developing a fuel reduction funding distribution tool, expected to be used for fiscal year 2016, which considers fire risks associated with each FWS unit. FWS officials told us this tool will identify risk reduction over longer periods of time, contain an accountability function to monitor results, and will share many attributes with FWS' preparedness allocation tool. NPS officials told us the agency will continue to rely on historical amounts, based largely on HFPAS. Similar to the previous Interior distribution approach, NPS distributes funding for specific projects identified at the headquarters level. However, if a unit is not able to implement an identified project, the unit can substitute other projects, as necessary.

CONCLUSION

Faced with the challenge of working to protect people and resources from the unwanted effects of wildland fire while also recognizing that fire is an inevitable part of the landscape, the federal wildland fire agencies have taken steps aimed at improving their approaches to wildland fire management. Their 2009 update to interagency guidance, for example, was designed to continue moving away from the agencies' decades-long emphasis on suppressing all fires, by giving fire managers more flexibility in responding to fires. In addition, the agencies are working to develop more up-to-date systems for distributing wildland fire resources. A central test of such changes, however, is the extent to which they help ensure appropriate and effective agency responses to fires when they occur. The agencies have acknowledged the importance of reviewing their responses to individual wildland fires to understand their effectiveness and identify possible improvements. However, the agencies have not systematically followed agency policy regarding such fire reviews and, in the reviews they have conducted, they have not used specific criteria in selecting fires and conducting the reviews. Officials from both the Forest Service and Interior told us cost alone should not be the basis for such reviews and have acknowledged the need to improve their criteria for selecting fires and conducting reviews. Draft guidance provided by the Forest Service did not contain specific criteria for such reviews, however, and Interior officials did not provide information about how they planned to develop criteria or the factors they would consider. By developing specific criteria for selecting fires to review and conducting the reviews, and making commensurate changes to agency policies to help ensure the criteria are consistently applied, the agencies may enhance their ability to ensure that their fire reviews provide useful information and meaningful results. This, in turn, could better position them to identify improvements in their approach to wildland fire management and thereby use their limited resources more effectively.

RECOMMENDATIONS FOR EXECUTIVE ACTION

To better ensure that the agencies have sufficient information to understand the effectiveness of their approach to wildland fires, and to better position them to develop appropriate and effective strategies for wildland fire management, we recommend that the Secretaries of Agriculture and the Interior direct the Chief of the Forest Service and the Director of the Office of Wildland Fire to take the following two actions:

- Develop specific criteria for selecting wildland fires for review and for conducting the reviews as part of their efforts to improve their approach to reviewing fires, and
- Once such criteria are established, revise agency policies to align with the specific criteria developed by the agencies.

AGENCY COMMENTS AND OUR EVALUATION

We provided a draft of this report for review and comment to the Departments of Agriculture and the Interior. The Forest Service (responding on behalf of the Department of Agriculture) and Interior generally agreed with our findings and recommendations. Both agencies stated that they are developing criteria for selecting fires to review and conducting reviews. Both agencies also provided technical comments which we incorporated into our report as appropriate. Interior also provided additional information about wildland fire technology, which we likewise incorporated as appropriate.

Anne-Marie Fennell
Director, Natural Resources and Environment

APPENDIX I: OBJECTIVES, SCOPE, AND METHODOLOGY

This report examines (1) key changes the federal wildland fire agencies have made in their approach to wildland fire management since 2009, (2) how the agencies assess the effectiveness of their wildland fire management programs, and (3) how the agencies determine the distribution of their wildland fire management resources.

To perform this work, we reviewed laws, policies, guidance, academic literature, and reviews related to federal wildland fire management. These included the 1995 Federal Wildland Fire Management Policy and subsequent implementation guidance, the *Interagency Standards for Fire and Fire Aviation Operations*, and the 2009 and 2014 Quadrennial Fire Reviews. We also interviewed headquarters officials from each of the five federal land management agencies responsible for wildland fire management—the Forest Service in the Department of Agriculture and the Bureau of Indian Affairs (BIA), Bureau of Land Management (BLM), Fish and Wildlife Service (FWS), and National Park Service (NPS) in the Department of the Interior—as well as Interior's Office of Wildland Fire.

We also conducted semistructured interviews of regional officials in each of the agencies to obtain information about issues specific to particular regions and understand differences across regions.[78] We interviewed wildland fire management program officials from each of the 9 Forest Service regional offices, 11 of BLM's 12 state offices,[79] and 2 regional offices each for BIA, FWS, and NPS. We focused these regional interviews primarily on the Forest Service and BLM because those agencies receive the greatest percentage of appropriated federal wildland fire funding. For BIA, FWS, and NPS, we selected the two regions from each agency that received the most funds in those agencies—BIA's Northwest and Western Regions, FWS's Southwest and Southeast Regions, and NPS's Pacific West and Intermountain Regions. We conducted a total of 25 semistructured interviews of regional offices.[80] During these semistructured interviews we asked about (1) significant changes to the agencies' approach to wildland fire management, including regional efforts to implement the policy areas identified in the *2009 interagency Guidance for Implementation of Federal Wildland Fire Management Policy*, (2) agency efforts to assess the effectiveness of their wildland fire management activities, and (3) agency processes for determining the distribution of fire management resources. We focused our review on three primary components of wildland fire management—suppression, preparedness, and fuel reduction—because they account for the highest spending amounts among wildland fire management activities.[81]

To address our first objective, we reviewed agency documents, such as policy and guidance, as well as other documents such as agency budget justifications, to identify changes the agencies have made to their approach to managing wildland fire since 2009, efforts the agencies have undertaken to address wildland fire management challenges, agency- identified improvements resulting from those changes, and challenges associated with implementing them. Our review focuses on changes since 2009 because we last completed a comprehensive review of wildland fire management in that year, and because the agencies' last significant change to interagency wildland fire management guidance for implementing the Federal Wildland Fire Management Policy also occurred that year. To further our understanding of these issues, we also asked about these changes in our interviews with agency headquarters officials. In particular, we asked about the extent to which changes to the agencies' wildland fire management approaches have occurred or are planned, the effects of these changes, and associated challenges. In addition, we relied on the semistructured interviews of regional officials described above to understand how the regions implemented national direction and policy. We analyzed the responses provided to us during the interviews to identify common themes about prominent changes since 2009, and challenges associated with implementing those changes. The information we report represents themes that occurred frequently in our interviews with both regional and headquarters officials. We did not report on changes described during our interviews that were not directly related to wildland fire management, such as changes to general workforce management policies.

To address our second objective, we reviewed agency strategic plans and budget justifications describing performance measures, as well as other documents associated with agency efforts to assess their programs, including fire reviews. We also reviewed legislative and agency direction related to fire reviews, including agency policies and the *Interagency Standards for Fire and Fire Aviation Operations*, and reviewed reports resulting from fire reviews conducted by the agencies since 2009. We compared agency practices for conducting fire reviews to direction contained in relevant agency policy. We also interviewed headquarters officials to identify the agencies' key performance measures and the extent to which those measures reflect changing approaches to wildland fire management. In our interviews with headquarters and regional officials, we also inquired about other mechanisms the agencies use to determine the effectiveness of their wildland fire management programs, as well as any changes they are making in this area. To obtain additional insight into the use of performance information on the part of federal agencies, we also reviewed our previous reports related to agencies' use of performance information.

To address our third objective, we reviewed relevant agency budget documentation, including annual budget justifications and documentation of agency obligations, as well as information about the tools and systems the agencies use to distribute funds and resources. We did not assess the design or use of any of the agencies' tools or systems for distributing funds. We interviewed agency officials at the headquarters and regional levels to identify the processes they use for budget formulation and resource distribution. We asked about the extent to which these processes have changed in recent years at the headquarters and regional levels for each of the five agencies and the extent to which they have changed funding and resource amounts. We also obtained data from the Forest Service and from Interior's Office of Wildland Fire on obligations for each of the three primary wildland fire management components— suppression, preparedness, and fuel reduction—from fiscal years 2004 through 2014, analyzing the data in both nominal (actual) and constant (adjusted for inflation) terms. Adjusting nominal dollars to constant dollars allows the comparison of purchasing power across fiscal years. To adjust for inflation, we used the gross domestic product price index with 2014 as the base year. We reviewed budget documents and obligation data provided by the agencies, and interviewed agency officials knowledgeable about the data, and we found the data sufficiently reliable for the purposes of this report.

We conducted this performance audit from August 2014 to September 2015 in accordance with generally accepted government auditing standards. Those standards require that we plan and perform the audit to obtain sufficient, appropriate evidence to provide a reasonable basis for our findings and conclusions based on our audit objectives. We believe that the evidence obtained provides a reasonable basis for our findings and conclusions based on our audit objectives.

APPENDIX II: FOREST SERVICE AND INTERIOR AGENCY OBLIGATIONS FOR PREPAREDNESS, FUEL REDUCTION, AND SUPPRESSION, FISCAL YEARS 2004 THROUGH 2014

This appendix provides information on preparedness, fuel reduction, and suppression obligations by the Forest Service and the Department of the Interior's four wildland fire agencies—the Bureau of Indian Affairs, Bureau of Land Management, Fish and Wildlife Service, and National Park Service—for fiscal years 2004 through 2014.

Figures 4, 5, and 6 show overall agency obligations for preparedness, fuel reduction, and suppression for fiscal years 2004 through 2014. Individual agencies' obligations for each of the three programs are described later in this appendix.

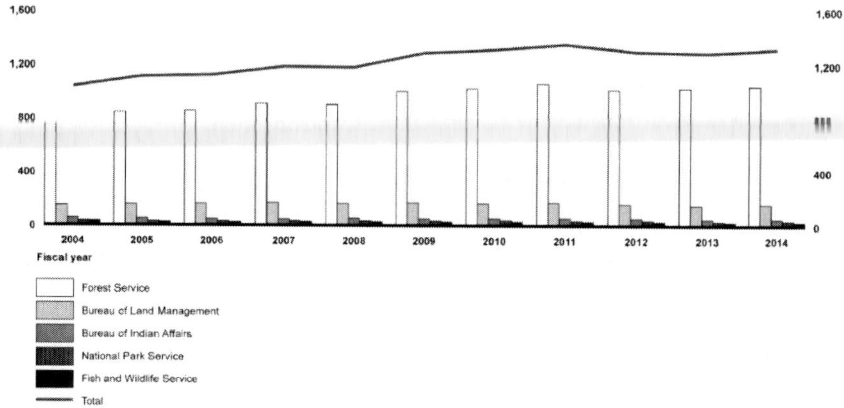

Sources: GAO analysis of Forest Service. Bureau of Land Management, Bureau of Indian Affairs, National Park Service, and Fish and wildlife Service funding data. |GAO-15-772

Figure 4. Forest Service and Interior Agency Wildland Fire Preparedness Obligations, Fiscal Years 2004 through 2014.

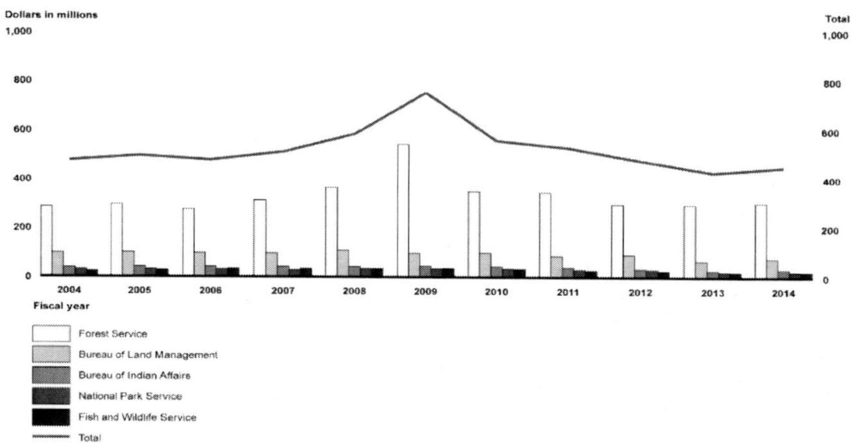

Sources GAO analysis of Forest Service. Bureau of Land Management, Bureau of Indian Affairs, National Park Service, and Fish and wildlife Service funding data. |GAO-15-772

Note: The increase in agency obligations for fuel reduction in fiscal year 2009 was due in part to additional appropriations provided by the American Recovery and Reinvestment Act of 2009 (Pub. L. No. 111-5).

Figure 5. Forest Service and Interior Agency Fuel Reduction Obligations, Fiscal Years 2004 through 2014.

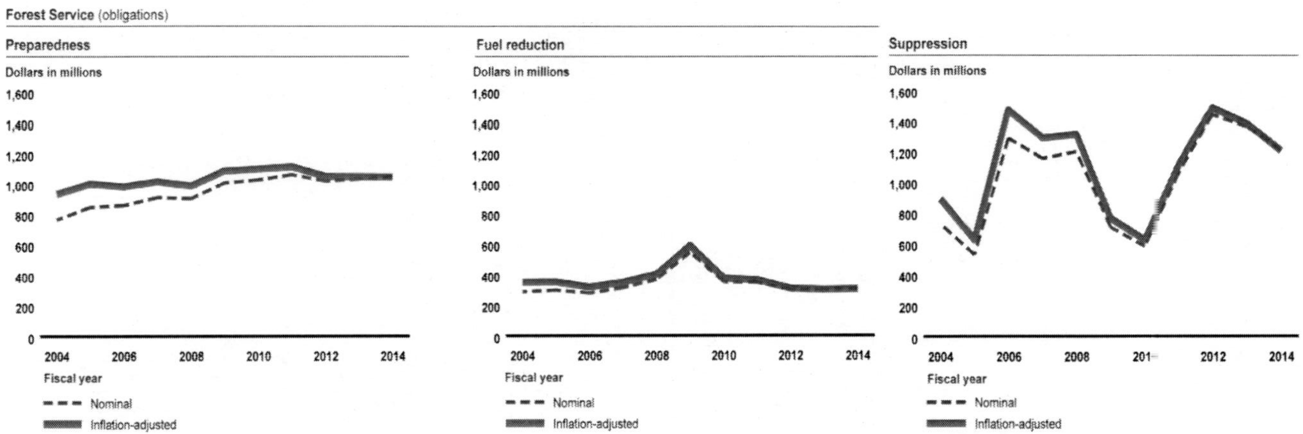

Source: GAO analysis of Forest Service funding data. | GAO-15-772
Note: Inflation-adjusted figures represent obligations in fiscal year 2014 dollars.

Figure 7. Forest Service Wildland Fire Obligations for Preparedness, Fuel Reduction, and Suppression, Fiscal Years 2004 through 2014.

Table 2. Bureau of Indian Affairs Wildland Fire Obligations for Preparedness, Fuel Reduction, and Suppression, Fiscal Years 2004 through 2014

Dollars in millions

	Preparedness		Fuel reduction		Suppression		Total	
Fiscal year	Nominal	Inflation- adjusted	Nominal	Inflation- adjusted	Nominal	Inflation- adjusted	Nominal	Inflation- adjusted
2004	$57.6	$70.3	$38.7	$47.2	$67.5	$82.4	**$163.8**	**$200.0**
2005	53.0	62.8	41.8	49.5	62.4	73.9	**157.3**	**186.2**
2006	48.5	55.6	41.7	47.8	82.9	95.1	**173.1**	**198.5**
2007	47.7	53.2	41.5	46.3	83.1	92.7	**172.2**	**192.2**
2008	55.0	60.1	41.7	45.6	87.9	96.2	**184.6**	**201.8**
2009	52.3	56.5	44.6	48.2	51.1	55.2	**147.9**	**159.9**
2010	54.4	58.3	43.2	46.3	43.2	46.3	**140.8**	**150.8**
2011	56.2	59.1	39.7	41.7	58.5	61.4	**154.5**	**162.2**
2012	54.8	56.6	33.0	34.0	105.4	108.7	**193.1**	**199.2**
2013	49.3	50.0	26.1	26.5	63.6	64.6	**139.0**	**141.2**
2014	50.8	50.8	29.7	29.7	53.2	53.2	**133.7**	**133.7**

Source: GAO analysis of Department of the Interior funding data. | GAO-15-772

Notes: Inflation-adjusted figures represent obligations in fiscal year 2014 dollars. Totals may not add due to rounding.

Table 3 and figure 9 show annual Bureau of Land Management wildland fire management obligations from fiscal years 2004 through 2014. Preparedness obligations increased from nearly $152 million in fiscal year 2004 to about $160 million in fiscal year 2014, an average annual increase of 0.6 percent per year, or a 1.4 percent decrease after adjusting for inflation. Fuel reduction obligations decreased from about $98 million in fiscal year 2004 to about $75 million in fiscal year 2014, an average annual decrease of 2.6 percent, or 4.6 percent after adjusting for inflation. Suppression obligations fluctuated from year to year, with a high of about $299 million in fiscal year 2007 and a low of about $130 million in fiscal year 2009.

Table 3. Bureau of Land Management Wildland Fire Obligations for Preparedness, Fuel Reduction, and Suppression, Fiscal Years 2004 through 2014

Dollars in millions								
	Preparedness		Fuel reduction		Suppression		Total	
Fiscal year	Nominal	Inflation-adjusted	Nominal	Inflation-adjusted	Nominal	Inflation-adjusted	Nominal	Inflation-adjusted
2004	$151.6	$185.1	$97.7	$119.3	$170.5	$208.1	**$419.8**	**$512.5**
2005	157.6	186.6	99.2	117.4	184.4	218.2	**441.2**	**522.2**
2006	162.2	185.9	97.2	111.4	262.7	301.2	**522.1**	**598.5**
2007	168.7	188.3	96.6	107.8	298.5	333.1	**563.8**	**629.3**
2008	163.3	178.6	109.4	119.6	198.0	216.5	**470.7**	**514.7**
2009	169.6	183.3	96.8	104.6	129.9	140.5	**396.3**	**428.3**
2010	166.2	178.0	98.3	105.4	160.0	171.4	**424.5**	**454.8**
2011	171.9	180.5	86.6	90.9	182.6	191.8	**441.1**	**463.3**
2012	161.1	166.2	91.8	94.7	292.2	301.3	**545.1**	**562.2**
2013	153.3	155.7	66.1	67.1	268.2	272.3	**487.6**	**495.1**
2014	160.2	160.2	74.8	74.8	211.3	211.3	**446.4**	**446.4**

Source: GAO analysis of Department of the Interior funding data. | GAO-15-772

Notes: Inflation-adjusted figures represent obligations in fiscal year 2014 dollars. Totals may not add due to rounding.

Table 4 and figure 10 show annual Fish and Wildlife Service wildland fire management obligations for fiscal years 2004 through 2014. Preparedness obligations decreased from about $33 million in fiscal year 2004 to about $27 million in fiscal year 2014, an average annual decrease of 2.1 percent per year, or 4.1 percent after adjusting for inflation. Fuel reduction obligations decreased from about $24 million in fiscal year 2004 to about $21 million in fiscal year 2014, an average annual decrease of 1.5 percent, or 3.5 percent after adjusting for inflation. Suppression obligations fluctuated from year to year, with a high of about $41 million in fiscal year 2011 and a low of about $4 million in fiscal year 2010.

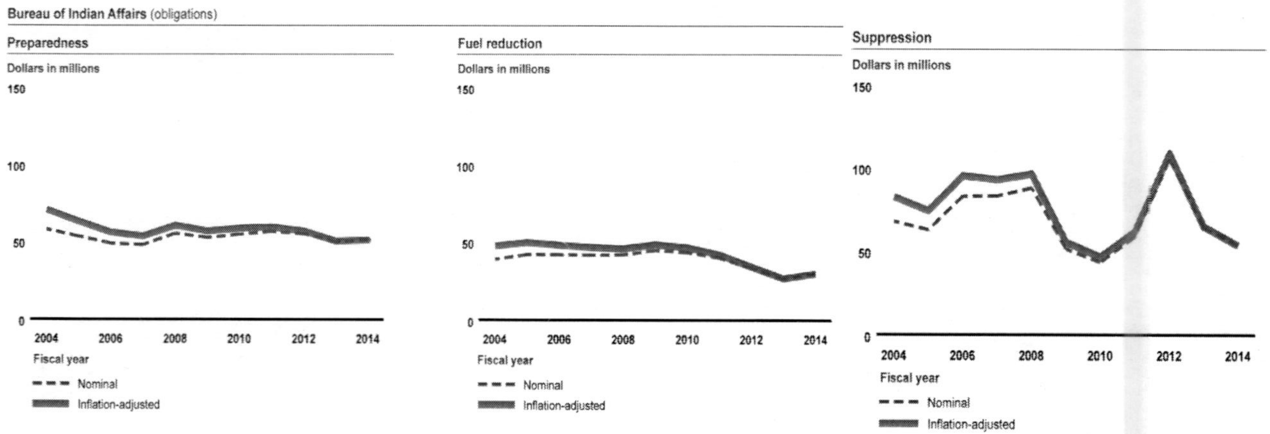

Source: GAO analysis of Department of the Interior founding data. |GAO-15-772
Note: Inflation-adjusted figures represent obligations in fiscal year 2014 dollars.

Figure 8. Bureau of Indian Affairs Wildland Fire Obligations for Preparedness, Fuel Reduction, and Suppression, Fiscal Years 2004 through 2014.

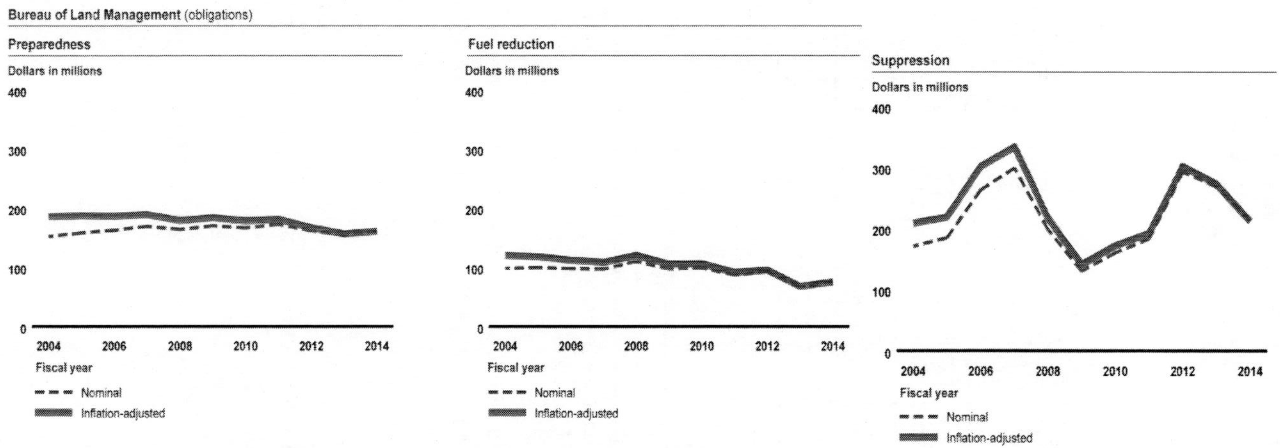

Source: GAO analysis of Department of the Interior founding data. | GAO-15-772
Note: Inflation-adjusted figures represent obligations in fiscal year 2014 dollars.

Figure 9. Bureau of Land Management Wildland Fire Obligations for Preparedness, Fuel Reduction, and Suppression, Fiscal Years 2004 through 2014.

Table 4. Fish and Wildlife Service Wildland Fire Obligations for Preparedness, Fuel Reduction, and Suppression, Fiscal Years 2004 through 2014

Dollars in millions

	Preparedness		Fuel reduction		Suppression		Total	
Fiscal year	Nominal	Inflation-adjusted	Nominal	Inflation-adjusted	Nominal	Inflation-adjusted	Nominal	Inflation-adjusted
2004	$33.4	$40.7	$24.2	$29.6	$8.4	$10.3	$66.0	$80.6
2005	26.8	31.7	27.9	33.0	14.3	16.9	69.0	81.7
2006	25.6	29.3	33.0	37.8	19.9	22.9	78.5	90.0
2007	27.7	30.9	33.0	36.8	31.4	35.1	92.1	102.8
2008	28.4	31.1	33.9	37.1	22.5	24.6	84.9	92.8
2009	28.2	30.5	34.8	37.6	15.0	16.2	78.0	84.4
2010	29.4	31.5	32.6	34.9	4.3	4.6	66.3	71.0
2011	29.0	30.4	27.5	28.8	40.5	42.6	97.0	101.8
2012	27.9	28.8	25.5	26.3	20.8	21.4	74.2	76.5
2013	25.9	26.3	20.2	20.5	14.1	14.3	60.2	61.1
2014	26.9	26.9	20.7	20.7	9.4	9.4	57.0	57.0

Source: GAO analysis of Department of the Interior funding data. | GAO-15-772

Notes: Inflation-adjusted figures represent obligations in fiscal year 2014 dollars. Totals may not add due to rounding.

Table 5 and figure 11 show annual National Park Service wildland fire management obligations for fiscal years 2004 through 2014. Obligations for preparedness increased from about $35 million in fiscal year 2004 to about $36 million in fiscal year 2014, an average annual increase of 0.5 percent per year, or a 1.5 percent decrease after adjusting for inflation. Fuel reduction obligations decreased from about $31 million in fiscal year 2004 to about $21 million in fiscal year 2014, an average annual decrease of 3.7 percent, or 5.6 percent after adjusting for inflation. Suppression obligations fluctuated from year to year, with a high of about $58 million in fiscal year 2006 and a low of about $22 million in fiscal year 2009.

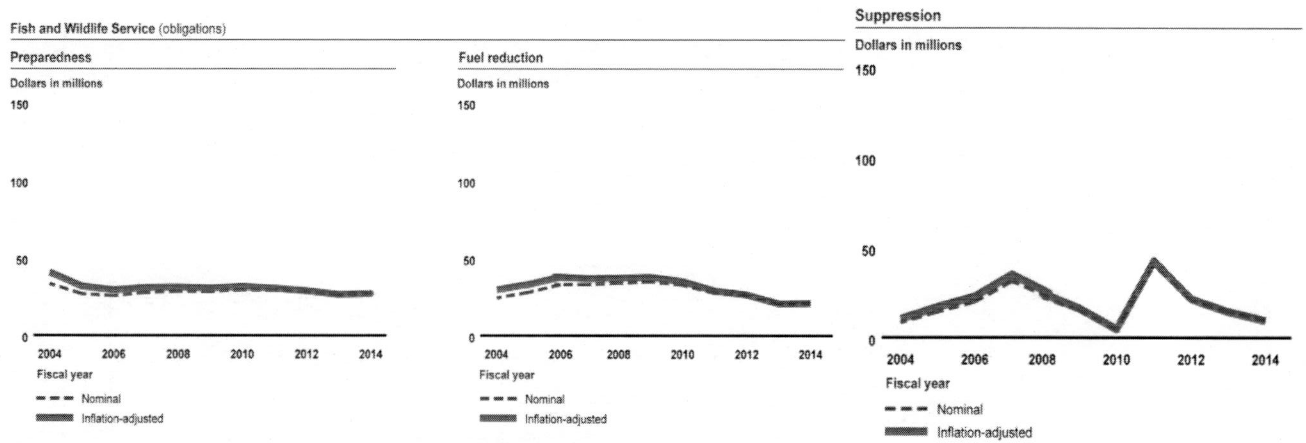

Source GAO analysis of Department of the Interior funding data. | GAO-15-772
Note: Inflation-adjusted figures represent obligations in fiscal year 2014 dollars.

Figure 10. Fish and Wildlife Service Wildland Fire Obligations for Preparedness, Fuel Reduction, and Suppression, Fiscal Years 2004 through 2014.

Table 5. National Park Service Wildland Fire Obligations for Preparedness, Fuel Reduction, and Suppression, Fiscal Years 2004 through 2014

Dollars in millions								
	Preparedness		Fuel reduction		Suppression		Total	
Fiscal year	Nominal	Inflation-adjusted	Nominal	Inflation-adjusted	Nominal	Inflation-adjusted	Nominal	Inflation-adjusted
2004	$34.6	$42.2	$31.1	$38.0	$34.9	$42.6	**$100.6**	**$122.8**
2005	31.5	37.3	31.8	37.7	32.9	39.0	**96.3**	**114.0**
2006	31.9	36.6	30.9	35.4	58.5	67.0	**121.2**	**139.0**
2007	34.1	38.1	28.6	31.9	57.4	64.1	**120.1**	**134.1**
2008	33.9	37.1	33.9	37.0	44.3	48.5	**112.1**	**122.6**
2009	34.4	37.2	33.9	36.6	22.4	24.2	**90.6**	**98.0**
2010	39.7	42.5	34.4	36.8	23.7	25.4	**97.8**	**104.7**
2011	36.4	38.2	30.3	31.8	37.0	38.9	**103.7**	**108.9**
2012	39.3	40.6	30.4	31.3	47.4	48.9	**117.1**	**120.8**
2013	31.0	31.5	21.0	21.3	53.1	53.9	**105.2**	**106.8**
2014	36.2	36.2	21.4	21.4	52.2	52.2	**109.8**	**109.8**

Source: GAO analysis of Department of the Interior funding data. | GAO-15-772

Notes: Inflation-adjusted figures represent obligations in fiscal year 2014 dollars. Totals may not add due to rounding.

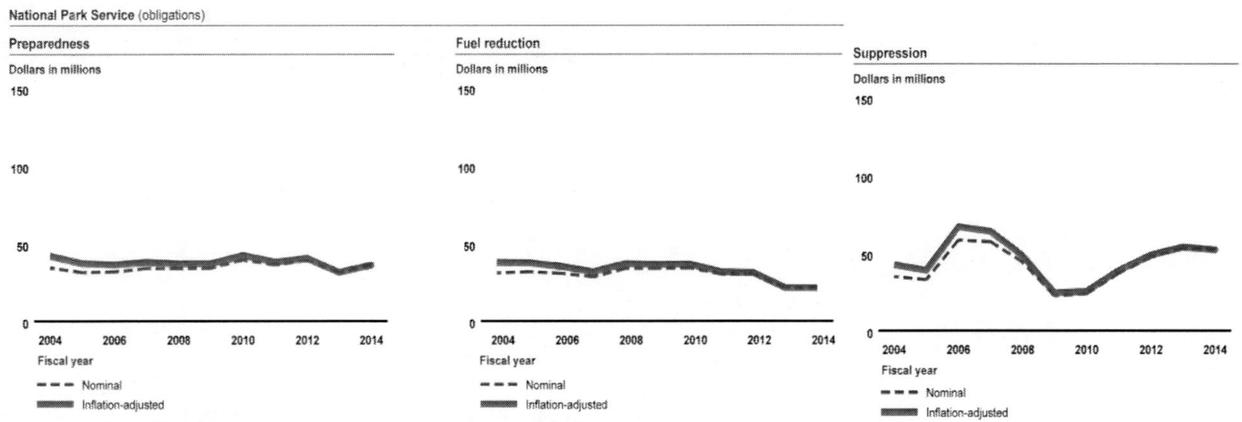

Source: GAO analysis of Department of the Interior funding data. | GAO-15-772
Note: Inflation-adjusted figures represent obligations in fiscal year 2014 dollars.

Figure 11. National Park Service Wildland Fire Obligations for Preparedness, Fuel Reduction, and Suppression, Fiscal Years 2004 through 2014.

APPENDIX III: DIFFERENCES IN FOREST SERVICE AND DEPARTMENT OF THE INTERIOR SALARY PAYMENTS USING PREPAREDNESS AND SUPPRESSION FUNDING

The Forest Service and the Department of the Interior use different approaches for paying the base salaries of their staff during wildland fire incidents.[83] For periods when firefighters are dispatched to fight fires, the Forest Service generally pays its firefighters' base salaries using *suppression* funds, whereas Interior pays its firefighters' base salaries primarily using *preparedness* funds.[84] Forest Service officials told us that under this approach, regional offices, which are responsible for hiring firefighters in advance of the fire season, routinely hire more firefighters than their preparedness budgets will support, assuming they can rely on suppression funds to pay the difference. Forest Service officials told us that their funding approach helps the agency maintain its firefighting capability over longer periods of time during a season and accurately track the overall costs of fires. Interior officials told us they choose to use preparedness funds to pay their firefighters' base salaries during a wildland fire because it constitutes a good business practice. According to a Wildland Fire Leadership Council document, in 2003, the council agreed that the agencies would use a single, unified approach and pay firefighters' base salary using Interior's method of using preparedness funds. However, the council subsequently noted that in 2004 the Office of Management and Budget directed the Forest Service to continue using suppression funds to pay firefighters' base salaries. The agencies have used separate approaches since 2004.

End Notes

[1] See, for example, National Research Council, *Climate Change: Evidence, Impacts, and Choices. Answers to Common Questions about the Science of Climate Change* (Washington, D.C.: 2012) and U.S. Climate Change Science Program, *The Effects of Climate Change on Agriculture, Land Resources, Water Resources, and Biodiversity in the United States* (Washington, D.C.: May 2008). The National Resource Council report notes that the risk of wildland fire is expected to increase in many regions, such as the evergreen forests of the western United States, and may decrease in other areas, such as those dominated by shrubs and grasses.

[2] Booz Allen Hamilton, *2014 Quadrennial Fire Review* (Washington, D.C.: May 2015). The Quadrennial Fire Review, prepared on behalf of the Forest Service and Interior, is a strategic assessment process conducted by the fire management agencies every 4 years to evaluate current wildland fire management strategies and capabilities against estimates of the future fire environment. The first such review occurred in 2005 and the second in 2009.

[3] See, for example, Department of Agriculture and Department of the Interior, *The National Strategy: The Final Phase in the Development of the National Cohesive Wildland Fire Management Strategy* (Washington, D.C.: April 2014), and Booz Allen Hamilton, *2014 Quadrennial Fire Review* (Washington, D.C.: May 2015).

[4] GAO, *Wildland Fire Management: Federal Agencies Have Taken Important Steps Forward, but Additional, Strategic Action Is Needed to Capitalize on Those Steps,* GAO-09-877 (Washington, D.C.: Sept. 9, 2009). For a list of GAO reports on topics related to federal wildland fire management, see the related products section at the end of this report.

[5] The Department of the Interior's Office of Wildland Fire organizes the activities of the four Interior agencies that manage and operate wildland fire programs. Specifically, it manages, oversees, and coordinates the department's wildland fire management programs, policies, budgets, information technology systems, and decision support tools.

[6] We did not interview officials from the BLM Eastern States Office because its wildland fire management program is minimal.

[7] The Forest Service, BIA, FWS, and NPS have regional offices, while BLM has state offices. For the purposes of this report, we refer to all of these as regional offices when we discuss the agencies collectively.

[8] An obligation is a definite commitment that creates a legal liability of the government for the payment of goods and services ordered or received, or a legal duty on the part of the United States. Payment may be made immediately or in the future. An agency incurs an obligation, for example, when it places an order, signs a contract, awards a grant, or purchases a service.

[9] See, for example, GAOand GAO, *Wildland Fire Management: Lack of Clear Goals or a Strategy Hinders Federal Agencies' Efforts to Contain the Costs of Fighting Fires*, GAO-07-655 (Washington, D.C.: June 1, 2007).

[10] The sagebrush steppe ecosystem is found in the western United States and western Canada. The sagebrush steppe name comes from the most dominant plant found in the ecosystem, the sagebrush, while steppe describes a largely treeless, dry, level grassland. According to BLM, the majority of BLM-managed lands are in the sagebrush steppe ecosystem.

[11] See, for example, National Research Council, *Climate Change: Evidence, Impacts, and Choices. Answers to Common Questions about the Science of Climate Change* (Washington, D.C.: 2012) and U.S. Climate Change Science Program, *The Effects of Climate Change on Agriculture, Land Resources, Water Resources, and Biodiversity in the United States* (Washington, D.C.: May 2008).

[12] Booz Allen Hamilton, *2014 Quadrennial Fire Review* (Washington, D.C.: May 2015). The states included in this statistic were Alaska, Arizona, California, Colorado, Idaho, Montana, Nevada, New Mexico, Oregon, Utah, Washington, and Wyoming.

[13] U.S. Global Change Research Program, *Climate Change Impacts in the United States: The Third National Climate Assessment* (Washington, D.C.: May 2014).

[14] These acts require the agencies to develop land management plans that provide for multiple uses. All land management actions must conform to the approved plan governing the land management unit—such as a national forest—where the action is to take place.

[15] The National Wildlife Refuge System Improvement Act of 1997 directs FWS to administer a national network of lands and waters for the conservation, management, and, where appropriate, restoration of the fish, wildlife, and plant resources and their habitats within the United States for the benefit of present and future generations of Americans. The National Park Service Organic Act of 1916 created the National Park Service to promote and regulate the use of national parks, monuments, and reservations with the purpose of conserving the scenery, natural and historic objects, and wildlife therein and to leave them "unimpaired" for the enjoyment of future generations.

[16] Booz Allen Hamilton, *2014 Quadrennial Fire Review* (Washington, D.C.: May 2015).

[17] The Firewise Communities program is a nonregulatory program administered by the National Fire Protection Association and sponsored by the Forest Service, Interior, and state forestry organizations. It is designed to involve homeowners, community leaders, planners,

developers, and others in efforts to protect people, property, and natural resources from the risk of wildland fire. Activities under the program include assisting individuals and residential communities with techniques to help protect homes and improve emergency preparedness in the event of wildland fire. Communities that take certain steps can become recognized as Firewise Communities sites. For more information on the program, see GAO, *Payments to Counties: More Clarity Could Help Ensure County Expenditures Are Consistent with Key Parts of the Secure Rural Schools Act*, GAO-12-775 (Washington, D.C.: July 16, 2012).

[18] Other fire program components include prevention; science, research, and development; site rehabilitation; and assistance to nonfederal entities.

[19] In 2015, Interior changed the name of its fuel reduction account to "fuel management" and now generally refers to this activity as fuel management rather than fuel reduction. However, for the purposes of this report, we refer to these activities and accounts collectively as fuel reduction.

[20] Department of Agriculture, Forest Service, Rocky Mountain Research Station, *Decision Making for Wildfires: A Guide for Applying a Risk Management Process at the Incident Level,* General Technical Report RMRS-GTR-298WWW (Ft. Collins, CO: June 2013).

[21] Values can include ecological, social, and economic values that could be lost or damaged due to fire, including people, property, infrastructure, natural and cultural resources, and air quality. Hazard is made up of the condition under which the fire burns, its ability to spread, and the intensity and severity it may present. For example, a fire that burns during extremely windy conditions may represent a greater hazard than a fire burning under less severe weather conditions. Probability is the likelihood of a fire becoming an active event and adversely affecting values, such as the likelihood that a fire will reach a particular point within a specified time period.

[22] David E. Calkin, Matthew P. Thompson, and Mark A. Finney, "Negative Consequences of Positive Feedbacks in U.S. Wildfire Management," *Forest Ecosystems*, vol. 2, no. 9 (2015).

[23] Pub. L. No. 60-136, 35 Stat. 259 (1908). This legislation also established that 25 percent of the revenue received from each national forest—through activities such as timber sales—must be paid to the relevant state for use on roads and schools in the counties where the national forest is located. 35 Stat. 260.

[24] Department of Agriculture, Forest Service, Pacific Northwest Research Station, *Ecological Foundations for Fire Management in North American Forest and Shrubland Ecosystems,* PNW-GTR-779 (March 2009).

[25] Administrative Policies for Natural Areas of the National Park System.

[26] The guidance states that the use of fire will be based on land or resource management plans and associated fire management plans prepared by individual units such as national parks. Land or resource management plans identify, among other things, fire's role in a particular area, and the objectives in the plans provide the basis for development of fire management objectives in designated areas. These fire-related objectives are contained in the units' fire management plans, which are intended to identify and integrate all wildland fire management and related activities within the context of approved land or resource management plans and assure that wildland fire management goals and components are coordinated.

[27] A fire regime describes the role fire plays in an ecosystem, including typical fire frequency, scale, intensity, and duration.

[28] The Federal Land Assistance, Management, and Enhancement (FLAME) Act of 2009 required the Forest Service and Interior to complete and submit to Congress a report that contains a "cohesive wildfire management strategy." Pub. L. No. 111-88 § 503, 123 Stat. 2971 (2009).

[29] The Federal Wildland Fire Management Policy of 1995, updated in 2001, urged coordination, consistency, and agreement not only among the five federal land management agencies but also between these agencies and other federal agencies as well as tribal, state, and private stakeholders.

[30] As part of the development of the Cohesive Strategy, each of three regions of the country—Northeast, Southeast, and Western—identified regional goals, objectives, and challenges to be incorporated into the national strategy, and the regions created implementation plans to help attain the goals.

[31] The Wildland Fire Leadership Council consists of senior officials from the Departments of Agriculture, Interior, and Homeland Security, including the Agriculture Undersecretary and Deputy Undersecretary for Natural Resources and Environment; the Interior Assistant Secretary for Policy, Management, and Budget; the Administrator of the U.S. Fire Administration; and the heads of the five federal firefighting agencies. Other members include representatives of the Intertribal Timber Council, the National Association of State Foresters, and the Western Governors' Association, along with a state forester and a local fire department chief.

[32] According to its website, the Nature Conservancy is a nonprofit organization that works to protect ecologically important lands and waters.

[33] The Forest Service is required to "in all ways that are practicable, aid in the enforcement of the laws of the States or Territories...for the prevention and extinguishment of forest fires[.]" 16 U.S.C. § 553. As noted in a 2006 report by the Department of Agriculture Inspector General, homeowner reliance on the federal government to provide suppression services in the WUI places a substantial financial burden on the Forest Service. Department of Agriculture, Office of Inspector General Western Region, *Audit Report: Forest Service Large Fire Suppression Costs*, Report No. 08601-44-SF (Washington, D.C.: November 2006).

[34] Cal. Pub. Res. Code § 4113.

[35] The Great Basin region includes parts of California, Idaho, Nevada, Oregon, and Utah. More than 350 species of plants and animals are found in this region.

[36] In 2011, FWS agreed to make a final listing decision concerning the greater sage- grouse by the end of fiscal year 2015.

[37] 75 Fed. Reg. 13910, 13982 (March 23, 2010).

[38] *Secretarial Order 3336, Rangeland Fire Prevention, Management, and Restoration*, January 5, 2015.

[39] https://wfdss.usgs.gov/wfdss/WFDSS_About.shtml, accessed August 10, 2015.

[40] Geospatial data describe features or phenomena that can be referenced to specific locations relative to the earth's surface. For example, features such as buildings, rivers, and federal lands, and phenomena such as wildland fires, can all be tracked by their geographic locations in data layers. These data layers can then be linked (or "layered") to display the combined information as maps with different layers of information, which may facilitate analysis of how the data in the various layers interrelate. See GAO, *Geospatial Data: Progress Needed on Identifying Expenditures, Building and Utilizing a Data Infrastructure, and Reducing Duplicative Efforts*, GAO-15-193 (Washington, D.C.: Feb. 12, 2015).

[41] Wildland Fire Lessons Learned Center, *Lessons From Recent Large Fire Reviews Briefing Paper* (August 7, 2013).

[42] We did not examine the agencies' information technology systems as part of this review.

[43] For large and complex fires, an incident management team comprising an incident commander and a cadre of personnel to handle command, planning, logistics, operations, and finance functions manages suppression operations. The incident management team orders firefighting assets—including personnel, aircraft, equipment, and supplies—through a three-tiered system of local, regional, and national dispatch centers.

[44] See, for example, Departments of Agriculture and the Interior, *2015 Direction to Wildland Fire Leadership* (Washington, D.C.: June 4, 2015), and Forest Service, *Chief's Letter of Intent – 2015 Fire Management* (Washington, D.C.: Jan. 28, 2015).

[45] We did not make a recommendation regarding this issue, noting that it would take several years, at the earliest, before the agencies could collect enough data for the model to be useful. See GAO

[46] Specifically, the index does not account for two of the main factors that influence suppression costs. These factors are long-term ecological conditions and changing climatic conditions, both of which may have substantial effects on fire management strategies. See Department of Agriculture, Forest Service, *Fiscal Year 2016 Budget Justification* (Washington, D.C.: February 2015).

[47] Interior officials told us this measure is based on information supplied by the field units responsible for the initial fire response, and that these units are responsible for determining whether the initial strategies succeeded.

[48] GAO, *Wildland Fire Management: Better Information and a Systematic Process Could Improve Agencies' Approach to Allocating Fuel Reduction Funds and Selecting Projects*, GAO-07-1168 (Washington, D.C.: Sept. 28, 2007) and GAO-09-877.

[49] See GAO

[50] Fuel Treatment Effectiveness Monitoring is a program to evaluate the effectiveness of prescribed fire and mechanical treatments designed to reduce the risk of wildfire. Forest Service and Interior agencies conduct assessments in instances where a wildfire either starts within or burns into a fuel treatment area, to evaluate the resulting impacts on fire behavior and fire suppression actions.

[51] The Interior agencies each issued their own guidance related to Fuel Treatment Effectiveness Monitoring. NPS issued guidance in 2012, BIA in 2013, BLM in 2014, and FWS in 2015.

[52] The Joint Fire Science Program is an interagency program that funds scientific research on wildland fires and distributes results to help policymakers, fire managers, and practitioners make sound decisions. The program is jointly funded by the Departments of Agriculture and the Interior and is governed by a 10-member board with 5 members from the Forest Service and 1 member each from BIA, BLM, FWS, NPS, and the U.S. Geological Survey. According to the program website, it has funded more than 170 studies examining the effectiveness of fuel reduction treatments in different locations since 1998.

[53] http://www.fs.fed.us/fire/aviation/afue/index.html, accessed July 31, 2015.

[54] In 2013, we recommended that the Forest Service and Interior expand efforts to collect information on aircraft performance and effectiveness to include all types of firefighting aircraft in the federal fleet, among other recommendations. See GAO, *Wildland Fire Management: Improvements Needed in Information, Collaboration, and Planning to Enhance Federal Fire Aviation Program Success*, GAO-13-684 (Washington, D.C.: Aug. 20, 2013).

[55] In some cases, those policies note that fire reviews may be conducted for other purposes, such as where the fire raised significant political, social, natural resource, or policy concerns.

[56] The Rim Fire burned about 154,000 acres of Forest Service land, about 79,000 acres of NPS land, and about 23,000 acres of private land.

[57] In June 2015, BLM issued guidance for reviewing fires occurring in sage-grouse habitat. The guidance calls for reviews of fires occurring during the 2015 wildland fire season on BLM-administered lands containing at least 10,000 acres of specifically designated sage- grouse habitat.

[58] Department of Agriculture Independent Large Fire Cost Review Panel and Guidance Group, Inc., *Large Fire Cost Review for Fiscal Year 2009* (August 2010).

[59] Wildland Fire Lessons Learned Center, *Lessons From Recent Large Fire Reviews Briefing Paper* (August 7, 2013). There was no similar analysis performed of the Forest Service's 10 reviews of fires occurring in 2013.

[60] See GAO, *Managing for Results: Enhancing Agency Use of Performance Information for Management Decision Making,* GAO-05-927 (Washington, D.C.: Sept. 9, 2005), GAO, *Nanotechnology: Improved Performance Information Needed for Environmental, Health, and Safety Research*, GAO-12-427 (Washington, D.C.: May 21, 2012), and GAO-13-684.

[61] As noted, the Forest Service allocates preparedness and fuel reduction funding directly to its nine regions, while Interior allocates funds to its four agencies, which in turn allocate to their respective regional offices. For both the Forest Service and the Interior agencies, once

regional offices receive funding, they in turn allocate funds to individual units such as national forests or national parks.

[62] As noted, values can include ecological, social, and economic values that could be lost or damaged due to fire, including people, property, infrastructure, natural and cultural resources, and air quality.

[63] As noted, unless otherwise specified, obligations are presented in nominal dollars, or actual dollars that are not adjusted for inflation.

[64] For example, to determine the fiscal year 2015 budget request for suppression, which the agencies submitted in fiscal year 2014, the agencies averaged obligations for suppression for fiscal years 2004 through 2013.

[65] See, e.g., Pub. L. No. 113–76, Div. G, Interior, Environment, and Related Agencies Appropriations Act, 2014, Title I, § 102, 128 Stat. 309 (Interior); Title III, 128 Stat. 325 (Forest Service).

[66] GAO, *Wildfire Suppression: Funding Transfers Cause Project Cancellations and Delays, Strained Relationships, and Management Disruptions*, GAO-04-612 (Washington, D.C.: June 2, 2004). In this report, we suggested that Congress consider alternative funding approaches for wildfire suppression to reduce the potential need for the Forest Service and Interior to rely on transferring funds from other programs to pay for wildfire suppression.

[67] Forest Service, *Fire Transfer Impact by State and Territory* (Washington, D.C.: June 2014).

[68] The remaining 1 percent of wildland fires typically account for the remaining 30 percent agencies spend on suppression, according to agency documents.

[69] For example, Title V of the Senate version of the Interior and Related Appropriations Act for Fiscal Year 2016 (S. 1645) would allow certain wildland fire suppression activities to be funded in a manner consistent with other natural disasters, using a modification of the approach proposed in the budget request.

[70] As noted, we did not assess the design or use of any of the agencies' tools or systems for distributing funds.

[71] Part of the difference in obligation amounts may be attributed to differences in how the Forest Service and Interior use preparedness funds to pay firefighters' salaries. See appendix III for more information about these differences.

[72] NFMAS had two primary components. One component provided historical weather and fire behavior data, and the other analyzed various fire-management scenarios, considering different combinations of firefighting resources, various potential wildfire conditions, and various resource values (such as the presence of timber or other commodity values), to help identify the most efficient level of preparedness resources for a given land management unit.

[73] Department of the Interior and Forest Service, *FPA Closeout and Transition Plan* (Washington, D.C.: September 29, 2014).

[74] Nevertheless, agency officials told us the effort resulted in some useful analytical products, including certain data sources and a large fire simulation modeling tool known as FSim.

[75] NPS officials told us they are working to refine their funding allocation process by combining results from the Planning Data System with outputs from a risk based fire occurrence and workload analysis tool that they are currently developing, the Strategic Allocation Model.

[76] As noted, Interior now refers to this activity as fuel management rather than fuel reduction.

[77] In 2007, we recommended that the agencies develop a systematic approach to allocating fuel reduction funding. See GAO

[78] The Forest Service, BIA, FWS, and NPS have regional offices, while BLM has state offices. For the purposes of this report, we refer to all of these as regional offices when we discuss the agencies collectively.

[79] We did not interview officials from the BLM Eastern States Office because its wildland fire management program is minimal.

[80] The number of semistructured interviews we conducted does not match the number of regional offices identified because two Forest Service regions were included in one interview.

[81] Other fire program components include prevention; science, research, and development; site rehabilitation; and assistance to nonfederal entities.

[82] According to Forest Service budget justifications, the Forest Service shifted aviation costs from the suppression account to the preparedness account beginning in fiscal year 2012. The Forest Service has retroactively adjusted the figures in both of these accounts for fiscal years 2005 through fiscal year 2011 to reflect this correction and allow comparability of numbers before and after this shift.

[83] Base salary represents the salary paid for a standard 8-hour work shift.

[84] Interior uses preparedness funds to pay for its firefighters' standard 8-hour work shift on a wildland fire, and suppression funds to pay for any overtime. The Forest Service uses suppression funds to pay for any time a firefighter spends on a wildland fire.

In: Federal Management of Wildland Fire ISBN: 978-1-63484-864-0
Editor: Rebecca Salazar

Chapter 2

STATEMENT OF TOM TIDWELL, CHIEF, USDA FOREST SERVICE. HEARING ON "THE FEDERAL GOVERNMENT'S ROLE IN WILDFIRE MANAGEMENT, THE IMPACT OF FIRES ON COMMUNITIES, AND POTENTIAL IMPROVEMENTS TO BE MADE IN FIRE OPERATIONS"*

INTRODUCTION

Madame Chairman and Members of the Committee, thank you for the opportunity to present the views of the USDA Forest Service regarding the Federal government's role in wildfire management, the impact of fires on communities, and potential improvements to be made in fire operations.

The United States and the rest of the world are experiencing heightened levels of wildfire activity. We are seeing wildfires in the United States grow to sizes that were unimaginable just 20 or 30 years ago. Many states including Florida, Georgia, Texas, Colorado, California, Oregon, Arizona, New Mexico, and Washington experienced either the largest and/or the most destructive fire in their history within the last seven years. Extreme wildfire threatens lives and the natural resources people need and value, such as clean, abundant

* This is an edited, reformatted and augmented version of a statement presented May 5, 2015 before the Senate Energy and Natural Resources Committee.

water; clean air; fish and wildlife habitat; open space for recreation; and other forest products and opportunities impacting the daily lives of many Americans.

We expect 2015 to continue the trend of above average fire activity. Our most recent forecast developed by Forest Service researchers at our Southern Research Station indicates there is a 90% chance that this year's fire suppression costs will be between $794M and $1.657B for the Forest Service, with a median estimate of $1.225B. The median is above the 10 year average and would certainly force us to transfer funding from other vital land management programs to support suppression operations.

The 2014 wildfire season was substantial, with over 60,000 wildfires in the United States that consumed over 3.5 million acres across all ownerships. Significant fire activity (fires over 40,000 acres) burned in Oregon, Washington, Alaska, Arizona, Idaho, and California. These fires affected watersheds for millions of people. Wildfire destroyed a total of 1,953 structures in 2014, including 1,038 residences. California accounted for the highest number of structures lost in one state in 2014 with over 300 dwellings destroyed.

The responsibility to respond to wildfire is not isolated to the Forest Service. We work extensively with our partners within the Department of the Interior (DOI) as well as State and local firefighting organizations to support wildland fire management operations. These cooperators are essential to ensuring that every wildfire receives an appropriate, risk informed, and effective response regardless of the jurisdiction. Not only does the Forest Service rely on our cooperators, but those cooperators rely on the Forest Service to meet their operational and land management objectives.

The entire wildland fire community has and will continue to utilize the National Cohesive Wildland Fire Strategy (Cohesive Strategy) to align priorities and define responsibilities across wildfire activities including prevention, fuels treatments and response. The Cohesive Strategy has three components that include: 1) restoring fire-adapted ecosystems, 2) building fire-adapted human communities, and 3) responding appropriately to wildfire.

PREPAREDNESS RESOURCES

The Forest Service and the DOI have the capability and responsibility to protect life, property, and natural resources while assuring an appropriate, risk-informed, and effective response to wildfires that is consistent with land and resource management objectives. We do this in close cooperation with States, Tribal governments, local governments, contract crews, and emergency/temporary hires. Firefighter and public safety are the primary considerations for all operations. The agencies continue to suppress approximately 98 percent of the fires on initial attack. However, the few fires that escape initial attack tend to grow quickly.

Within the FY2015 appropriation for Wildland Fire Management, we will be able to sustain comparable levels of firefighting assets as we have in previous years. We are able to leverage Call-When-Needed (CWN) aviation and ground based assets as the situation requires. We also coordinate with other Federal, State and local partners to maximize the utility of the community of assets to ensure we are able to respond when levels of fire activity increase. Approximately 10,000 firefighters from the Forest Service and 3,200 DOI firefighters are available for the upcoming fire season.

An integral component of our readiness is aviation resources. This year, we will have up to 21 airtankers available for operations on exclusive use contracts including: six legacy airtankers, up to 14 next generation tankers, and one agency owned/contractor operated HC-130H. The Forest Service also expects to have airtankers available through CWN contracts as well as the capability to mobilize cooperator airtankers if available through agreements with the state of Alaska and Canada. In addition, in 2015, the Forest Service will have available for wildfire suppression nationwide one CL415 Water Scooper through an exclusive use contract and one Single Engine Airtanker available through a shared Bureau of Land Management/ Forest Service exclusive use contract. The DOI additionally has 70 Single Engine Airtankers and four Water Scoopers to support wildfire response in situations where a smaller aircraft is the most effective tool. In coordination with the military, there are up to eight Mobile Airborne Firefighting System (MAFFS) capable C-130H available to meet surge requirements. We also have an extensive fleet of over 100 helicopters available to support response operations and 42 providing support from the DOI agencies.

The Forest Service continues to implement the 2012 Large Airtanker Modernization strategy that identifies the need for next generation tankers that have expanded capability and increased retardant delivery capacity. We have made progress modernizing our airtanker fleet with the impending transfer of the seven HC-130Hs from the Coast Guard, the upcoming acquisition of a next generation airtanker and the exclusive use contracting of up to 14 next generation airtankers. We have implemented several initiatives including the Aerial Firefighting Use and Effectiveness Program (AFUE) to help us better understand the best mix and use of our aviation assets to meet the changing conditions and operational requirements of wildfire response. AFUE will assist in establishing performance metrics and operational guidelines to improve our response capabilities and safety of our operators.

It is just as important to have substantial pre-seasonal planning operations occur with our cooperators and adjacent communities as it is to have our assets trained and ready to respond. The goal of building fire-adapted human communities provides context for our relationship with our cooperators and the public. We work to establish reasonable expectations as well as how the community can help be better prepared for wildland fire by participating in programs like Fire Wise, Fire Adapted Communities, creating Community Wildland Fire Protection Plans and implementing other mitigation and resiliency projects to offset and minimize the inherent risk that wildfire poses.

SUPPRESSION

Over the last few decades, wildfire suppression costs have increased as fire seasons have grown longer and the frequency, size, and severity of wildfires has increased due to changing climatic conditions, drought, hazardous fuel buildups, insect and disease infestations, nonnative invasive species, and other factors. These trends are expected to continue. Over the last 10 years, adjusting for inflation, the Forest Service has spent an average of almost $1.13 billion on suppression operations annually. The Department of the Interior agencies adjusted suppression obligations for the same period is $383.7 million. This change is attributed to many factors including increased development in the wildland urban interface, degraded ecological conditions, and a changing climate. There has been an increase in frequency of large catastrophic fires in which we expend significant financial resources.

We manage suppression costs by utilizing the best available information and applying the right resource at the right place, at the right time, for the right duration with the right plan. The largest fires we manage often present extraordinary attributes that create risks to people and other high valued assets that are difficult and costly to manage. We believe that by continuing to apply risk management principles, decisions will be made that not only provide an appropriate, risk informed and effective response to all wildfires, but also ensure that costs are commensurate with the values at risk.

The Forest Service and the DOI determined that 1 percent of fires consume about 30 percent of the wildfire suppression budget. The

Administration believes these types of wildfires should be considered natural disasters and treated as such for funding purposes. Unlike other Federal agencies responsible for responding to natural disasters, the Forest Service is required to fund its entire emergency management program through its regular appropriated discretionary budget.

The President's FY 2016 budget includes a proposal to reform the way that wildfire suppression is funded. The Administration's proposal aligns with the Wildfire Disaster Funding Act introduced this Congress. The reforms contained in these proposals are necessary and vital to ensure the Forest Service and the DOI are able to continue to deliver the full scope of their missions. Since FY 2002, the Forest Service has transferred funds from non-fire accounts seven times. In the same time period, the DOI has had to transfer funds to cover suppression obligations six times. Transferring funds to cover the cost of wildfire suppression is disruptive and harmful to other critical Forest Service and DOI programs and services, including efforts to reduce wildfire risk through mechanical thinning, prescribed fires, and other means.

Even in years when the Forest Service does not transfer funds from other programs the uncertainty created by the possibility of "fire transfer" means key projects, including those that contribute to forest health and hazardous fuels reduction, are put on hold in anticipation of a high wildfire activity year.

HAZARDOUS FUELS

Decades of fire suppression and other factors have led to increases of fuels in many forest types across the country. Treating these acres through commercial thinning, hazardous fuels removal, re-introduction of low-intensity fires and other means can reduce fuel loads, provide forest products to local mills, provide jobs to local communities, and improve the ecological health of our forests and rangelands.

Fifty-eight million acres of national forests are at high or very high risk of severe wildfire. Out of the 58 million "high or very high" risk acres, we have identified approximately 11.3 million acres for highest priority treatment. These acres are in proximity to the wildland-urban interface or are in priority watersheds or water sources, are in frequent fire return regimes, and are not in roadless or wilderness areas.

Together with our partners in fire management, including Federal, State, local, tribal, nongovernmental, academia and landowner organizations, the Forest Service and DOI have worked collaboratively to develop the Cohesive

Strategy of which fuel treatment is an essential component. Fuel treatments result in better outcomes on the land: more resilient, healthier ecosystems that provide the many benefits society wants and needs.

We control fuels in the wildland/urban interface (WUI) by removing buildup of dead vegetation and thinning over dense forests. We focus on treating high-priority areas, including municipal watersheds to protect water supplies. In FY2014, the Hazardous Fuels program treated more than 2.5 million acres on National Forest System and adjacent lands both inside and outside the WUI. The Hazardous Fuels program utilizes a decision support system called the Hazardous Fuels Priority Allocation System (HFPAS) to inform allocation decisions. Within HFPAS an assessment is completed that determines the likelihood that high intensity wildfires will intersect with residential areas and municipal water supplies. The results of the HFPAS analysis are combined with other treatment and ecological objectives to inform the allocations. In 2015, we funded nationally competitive projects that will reduce the risk to communities and firefighters and increase the resilience of the forests. In addition, these projects target areas of high risk near communities that are actively working to reduce the fire risk to their community.

There are many other programs within the Forest Service that also reduce the risk of catastrophic wildland fires including the Collaborative Forest Landscape Restoration Program (CFLR). The CFLR assists in the agency's work with partners to conduct hazardous fuel treatments and ecosystem restoration that encourage economic and social sustainability, leverage local resources with national and private resources, reduce wildfire management costs, and address the utilization of forest restoration byproducts to offset treatment costs and benefit local economies. The CFLR uses a competitive process to select projects which foster collaborative, science-based restoration on priority forest landscapes across the Nation. Although CFLR is not the only program that contributes to this goal, the relationships the agency builds through this program provides models for how community partnerships can help advance landscape restoration efforts. In FY 2014, CFLR projects delivered substantial progress in restoring ecosystem resilience and reducing the risk of uncharacteristic wildland fire.

Since the first CFLR projects began implementation, the Forest Service has worked with partners to accomplish over 1.45 million acres of hazardous fuels treatments in the 23 project areas to reduce the risk of catastrophic wildfire. Approximately 870,100 of these acres treated were within the wildland-urban interface and 509,200 acres were outside of the interface.

The Forest Service's wood utilization program develops markets to reduce the cost of hazardous fuels treatments, forest management, and restoration activities. The USDA Wood to Energy Initiative is an interagency effort to expand renewable wood energy development and use. In FY 2015, the Forest Service awarded over 40 Wood Innovation Grants to communities, businesses, Tribes, States, and other organizations to help expand and accelerate wood energy and wood products markets through the country. The National Forest System is an important source of woody biomass and many of the CFLR projects are actively pursuing the development of woody biomass utilization opportunities. The National Forest System made 2.2 million tons of woody biomass available through the use of stewardship, logging, and other contracting authorities in FY 2014.

In the past four years, the USDA Wood to Energy Initiative resulted in more than 270 projects, roughly $1 billion in USDA loans and grants, and increased private sector leverage for wood energy projects. In FY 2014, State and Private Forestry awarded $1.25 million in grants for wood energy projects and $2.5 million in cooperative agreements to establish 11 Statewide Wood Energy teams. The Forest Service also invested $3 million in strategic alliances that successfully leveraged substantial non-Federal funding for wood energy initiatives in FY 2014.

The DOI is appreciative of the $10 million in funding appropriated by Congress in FY 2015 to pilot the Resilient Landscapes program. The new program is a place-based, collaborative approach critical to the Interior agencies in meeting the Cohesive Strategy goal of restoring and maintaining landscapes across all jurisdictions that are resilient to fire related disturbances in accordance with management objectives. Interior received 29 proposals representing a variety of ecosystems across the United States and inclusive of many different, agencies, tribes, and partners. The selection process should be concluded by the end of May. Selected proposals will begin restoring fire resiliency across landscapes this year, leveraging wildland fire management funds and efforts with agency resource management programs and partners.

In closing, we anticipate another active fire year as above normal wildland fire potential exists across the north central United States this spring while above normal wildland fire potential continues to threaten many parts of the West this summer. We look forward to the safe return of the brave men and women who serve on the front lines of protecting life and property during this year's fire season. We appreciate the introduction of the Wildfire Disaster Funding Act that will help the Forest Service and DOI avoid the need to transfer funds from other agency programs to pay for suppression.

Finally, we welcome the opportunity work with the committee to identify ways to accomplish additional work to reduce the threat of fire by restoring the Nation's forests and rangelands.

In: Federal Management of Wildland Fire ISBN: 978-1-63484-864-0
Editor: Rebecca Salazar

Chapter 3

STATEMENT OF STEPHEN J. PYNE, PROFESSOR & DISTINGUISHED SUSTAINABILITY SCHOLAR SCHOOL OF LIFE SCIENCES, ARIZONA STATE UNIVERSITY. HEARING ON "THE FEDERAL GOVERNMENT'S ROLE IN WILDFIRE MANAGEMENT, THE IMPACT OF FIRES ON COMMUNITIES, AND POTENTIAL IMPROVEMENTS TO BE MADE IN FIRE OPERATIONS"*

Good morning. I'm a professor in the Human Dimensions faculty, School of Life Sciences, Arizona State University. What I have to say is the result of 48 years associated with wildland fire in some capacity or other. Most recently, with funding from the Forest Service, DoI, and Joint Fire Science Program, I have been writing a history of wildland fire in America since 1960.

Modern fire management effectively began in the aftermath of the Great Fires of 1910. The Big Blowup traumatized the fledgling Forest Service and its chiefs for decades. One of the aftershocks, the 1911 Weeks Act, established

* This is an edited, reformatted and augmented version of a statement presented May 5, 2015 before the Senate Energy and Natural Resources Committee.

the basis for a national infrastructure with the U.S. Forest Service as the institutional matrix.

For the next 50 years the country pursued a strategy of fire exclusion, so far as possible. The Forest Service connected federal agencies and states. It was a policy of *resistance* - that is, it sought to eliminate the fire threat by attacking every fire before it could become big, a kind of forward strategy. Part of the appeal of the policy was its administrative clarity and unblinking rules of engagement that mandated control by 10 am the morning following a fire's discovery. By 1960 the Forest Service had become a benign hegemon that controlled nearly every aspect of wildland fire and much of the rural fire scene.

This approach proved useful for rapidly building out a national system. It failed, however, as a universal strategy because it proved impossible to abolish fire, because those fires that did escape initial attack only became bigger, and because many landscapes suffered from a lack of fire. The strategy eliminated good fires as well as bad ones. It forced one agency to absorb and resolve all the tensions regarding how the national estate should be managed.

In the 1960s a new strategy of *restoration* emerged. It sought to reinstate the good fires lost under the previous regime, it wanted a more pluralistic oversight of policy than that provided by the Forest Service, and it nurtured a civil society to counter what was becoming a de facto government monopoly. Critically, it was not enough to have a stand-alone fire protection program: fire had to be integrated with land management. Over the next 15 years every federal land agency had its mission rechartered. As the purpose of those lands changed, so did their requirements for fire.

The first salvos in this fire revolution came in 1962. By 1968 the National Park Service had recanted the 10 am policy in favor of restoration; in 1978 the Forest Service achieved a complete overhaul of its fire mission and its financing. The new strategy pivoted around a concept of fire by prescription. Good fires would be introduced deliberately on working landscapes, and natural fires would be granted more room to do their ecological work in wild landscapes; both kinds of fire would be conducted under a specified set of guidelines called a prescription. Meanwhile, interagency organizations supplemented and then replaced the Forest Service as an overseer, and then they expanded from interagency programs to intergovernmental ones, and now they include NGOs and the private sector as well. The collapse of the old order was remarkably swift. It was like watching the Berlin Wall fall overnight. Or less dramatically, like watching the breakup of AT&T's telephone monopoly which happened at the same time.

The new strategy has now run its own 50-year course, and its problems and promises have sharpened. Prescribed burning has proved more a regional than a national project. It works as a foundational doctrine in the southeast and parts of the Great Plains - though no one seems to get as much burning done as they believe they need - but it has not become a routine operation in the West or Alaska. The prescribed natural fire died as a concept after the 1988 Yellowstone fires, though it continues to be reincarnated in other avatars.

The fire revolution overall stalled during the 1980s. The reasons are many; some within the purview of the American fire community, many not. Reforms renewed after the 1994 season, culminating in a common federal wildland fire policy (1995) and the National Fire Plan (2000). The project has had its successes and showcase programs, but the sad fact remains that the reformation in fire management has not achieved anything like the dimensions projected or needed. Most observers consider that the threats are outpacing our responses. Moreover, the institutional scene has been overwhelmed by competing purposes and new organizations including local-jurisdiction and volunteer fire departments, a gamut of NGOs from the Nature Conservancy to National Coalition of Prescribed Fire Councils, and private companies which have grown on such a scale that critics now speak of a fire-industrial complex.

Which leads to a consideration of what the next 50 years might hold. A new strategy seems to be congealing in the West that we might label *resilience*. It accepts that we aren't going to get ahead of the problem overall, that too many variables are in motion, that the fire community controls too few of those causes to intervene in fundamental ways. It seeks to make the best of the hand we are being dealt, even if, paradoxically, American society is the dealer.

These three historical eras underwrite the three general strategies in play today.

Resistance. There remains an Old Guard from the 1960s who would like a return to the former order, and there are more contemporary thinkers who want to transform wildland fire organizations into an all-hazard emergency service, effectively urban fire departments in the woods, or at a national level, a kind of Coast Guard for the interior.

This is happening globally, motivated by desires to protect structures and lives. Evidence to date suggest that such a revival or a repurposing can help attend to a threatened public but it has not shown it can manage fire because it breaks the bond between fire management and land management. If it retains the strengths of fire suppression, it also retains suppression's formidable weaknesses as a singular strategy.

Restoration. Restoration remains an inspirational goal for many practitioners, either to return to a golden age in the past or to advance toward one in the future. Its motivation is a near-universal unhappiness with the existing scene. But restoration, too, has upgraded its mission to include complex collaborations, ways to supplement prescribed fire with other treatments, and a determination to get ahead of the problem, to gather and apply the best science in order to restructure the national estate in such a way that we can control bad fires and reintroduce good fires more easily, cheaply, and safely.

There are many projects actively underway. Yet if its vision still shines brightly, so, too, its problems continue to darken. It has proved costly, not only in money but in political and social capital. Research, reviews, NEPA protocols, endless conversations among stakeholders - these are a necessary exercise in democracy but can take years. Moreover, the actual area involved is small relative to the size of the challenge. The threats are growing bigger and faster than our responses. We need flexibility to operate on landscape scales, not only geographically but institutionally. We need to move beyond single projects and events. There is little reason to believe that the country will muster the will to rehabilitate at the rate or scale required the 39-58 million acres believed out of whack.

Resilience. In the West a strategy is emerging that accepts, in fact if not in doctrine, that we cannot get ahead of the problems coming at us. Instead, it allows for the management of wildland fires to shift, where possible, from attempts at direct control to more indirect reliance on confining and containing outbreaks. Of course there are fires that simply bolt away from the moment of ignition. But many fires offer opportunities to back off and burn out. It is hoped that this strategy will prove more cost effective and safer for fire crews, while introducing some degree of semi-controlled ecological burning. These are not let-burns. Rather, fire officers concentrate their efforts at point protection where assets are most valuable such as communities, municipal watersheds, or sequoia groves. Elsewhere they will try to pick places - draw boxes - which they can hold with minimum costs, risks, and damages. A given fire might see aggressive firefighting on one flank, or on one day, and a more removed burning out on another flank or at another time.

The strategy is compatible with federal policy, and in many respects moves in directions long urged by critics and even the GAO, though it can look like a mashup and the outcomes will be mixed. Some patches will burn more severely than we would like (maybe 15-20%?), and some will barely burn at all (another 15-20%?), but the rest will likely burn within a range of tolerance. Such burnouts may well be the future of prescribed fire in the West. If so we need to do them better, and we need to understand how to build future landscapes out of the patchy aftermath of the megafires that characterize the current regime.

Equally, we need a reordering of the institutional landscape. In political terms we are witnessing the American fire community's euro moment. We either truly integrate, or we break up, or we tolerate endless bailouts. The National Cohesive Strategy could become the start of a kind of fire constitution that redefines for our federal system the roles, rights, and responsibilities of the many, many players in the American way of fire. It could do for the future what the Weeks Act did after the Big Blowup.

So, three strategies. It's worth pointing out that all fire strategies suffer failures and at roughly the same rate. Some 2-3% of wildfires escape initial attack. Rough estimates suggest a comparable number of prescribed fires escape or fail to do the ecological work expected. And we can expect similar breakdowns with landscape restoration.

Without wishing to sound flip or push an analogy too closely, we might call the resistance strategy a rock, the restoration strategy a scissors, and the resilience strategy a paper. At any given time and place one trumps another and is itself trumped. All three remain in play, and all three are needed. We need rocks around our prize assets and communities when they are threatened by going fires. We need scissors to buffer against bad burns and nudge toward good ones as part of managing healthy land. And we need resilience because the ideal can be the enemy of the good, and a mixed strategy that includes boxing-and-burning may be the best we can hope for.

Thank you.

In: Federal Management of Wildland Fire
Editor: Rebecca Salazar
ISBN: 978-1-63484-864-0

Chapter 4

TESTIMONY OF DR. THOMAS ZIMMERMAN, PRESIDENT, INTERNATIONAL ASSOCIATION OF WILDLAND FIRE. HEARING ON "FEDERAL AGENCY WILDFIRE MANAGEMENT"*

Good Morning, I would like to thank Senators Cantwell and Barrasso and the Committee for the opportunity to appear here today and provide input to its Hearing on *Opportunities to Improve the Organizational Response of the Federal Agencies in the Management of Wildland Fires.*

My name is Thomas Zimmerman and I am here in the capacity of President and Chairman of the Board of the International Association of Wildland Fire (IAWF). I am also a member of the Association for Fire Ecology and the Society of American Foresters. I served in a variety of wildland fire management positions with the Bureau of Land Management, National Park Service, and most recently, the U.S Forest Service until 2012. Since retirement, I have been involved in natural resource consulting. My career spanned 40 years and included positions throughout the organization at all levels and in leadership positions at the field, state, regional, and national levels. I have also earned a Ph.D. Fire Science.

The topic of today's hearing is perfectly aligned with the vision and purpose of the IAWF and very important to both myself, and our membership.

---

* This is an edited, reformatted and augmented version of testimony presented August 27, 2015 for a Seattle field hearing of the Senate Energy and Natural Resources Committee.

We are a non-profit, professional association representing members of the global wildland fire community. We were established 25 years ago and strive to:

- Facilitate communication and provide leadership for the wildland fire community.
- Promote a better understanding of wildland fire,
- Facilitate wildland fire management knowledge and education,
- Advance science and technology,
- *And build on the belief that an understanding of his dynamic force is vital for natural resource management, for firefighter safety, and for harmonious interaction between people and their environment.*

The unfolding of events during this year's fire season have been truly unfortunate and tragic. It is with great sadness that we proceed knowing that all the firefighters that started this season will not be able to finish it. The heartbreaking loss of life we have recently witnessed brings emotions that are beyond description. Our hearts and prayers go out to all the families and friends of our fallen colleagues.

As the field of wildland fire management moves forward, it seems that the interrelated factors influencing it continue to add complexity. Fire occurrence and response now constitute a year-round activity; fire numbers are increasing; seasonal burning periods are extending; and response capabilities are heavily taxed. Whether it is fire environment properties or social, political, and ecological elements, the challenges of the fire management program continue to mount.

But on a number of fronts, we should consider ourselves well positioned to move into the future. Wildland fire management as a professional land management program has progressed greatly over the last century. Our knowledge of certain fire management areas such as the natural role of fire; fire behavior and fire effects; science, technology, and operational capabilities; policy dynamics; and management strategies and tactics has never been greater. We know that:

- Fire influences and initiates ecological and social processes,
- Fires will occur with differential fire behavior and differential patterns and cause differential effects,
- Vegetation and fuel complexes are changing,

- Human management of fire, regardless of objectives, has both intended and unintended influences on ecosystems,
- Climate change is and will continue to affect fire and ecosystem dynamics,
- Wildland–urban interface areas are enlarging,
- Social dynamics are having an increasing influence on fire management activities,
- Smoke management has become an important decision consideration,
- Managing resource values and sustaining fire dependent ecosystems is a critical goal, and
- Collaboration and communication are vital to planning and implementation.

Even so, the future of wildland fire management cannot be predicted with a high degree of reliability and there is little doubt that we have entered a very transformative time. The 2015 wildfire season is one of the most severe in recent years and serves as a case in point. To date, wildfires have burned more than 7.5 million acres -- more than double the number of acres burned last fire season -- destroying lives, homes and precious natural and cultural resources. In the face of this natural disaster, the Federal Government, working with states and local communities, and with international assistance, is mounting a full-force response. Unfortunately, wildfires continue to burn in the West, with little to no relief in sight for the immediate future, and the season is far from over.

The National Preparedness level remains at its highest state, and the National Multi-Agency Coordinating (NMAC) group is deploying a record number of Federal firefighting resources. In addition, two hundred soldiers from Fort Lewis, Washington, and international air and ground resources from Australia, Canada and New Zealand are bolstering our wildland firefighting resources.

It is easy for managers to highlight program elements where needs seem logical. Frequently identified areas include strategic thinking, budget levels, staffing and equipment levels, technology, information management, research, training, decision-making, management focus, and predicting the future. However, determining innovative solutions is difficult; resistance to change is hard to overcome, and precedence tends to push us to familiar ways of doing business. To meet future challenges, problems must be clearly defined, understood, and parceled into achievable divisions.

Guiding Framework for Wildland Fire Management: The framework of information, representing policy, strategic plans, and program reviews provides in-depth information and guidance to the wildland fire management program. This information frames program planning and implementation and carries far greater value than ever before. It allows for greater flexibility, keeps pace with a dynamic situation, and embodies the state of the knowledge, the state of the art, and latest science and technology.

- Wildland fire management policy. Fire policy has been quite responsive to changing situational dynamics. It has progressed to a point where decision-makers have more flexibility than at any previous time. Accepted strategies are more sophisticated and comprehensive and tactical spectrums fully support a wider range and multiple objectives. The current policy is adequate and remains consistent with the growing awareness that future program needs cannot be accomplished solely by a passive approach that places an over-reliance on past practices, processes, and applications.

Two source documents describe the federal wildland fire management policy. These are:

- 1995 Federal Wildland Fire Management Policy and Program Review: http://www.forestsandrangelands.gov/strategy/documents/foundational/1995 fed wildland fire policy program report.pdf , and
- 2009 Guidance for Implementation of Federal Wildland Fire Management Policy: https://www.nifc.gov/policies/policiesdocuments/GIFWFMP.pdf

The 1995 policy document created a foundation still valid today and presents nine guiding principles, which include:

- Firefighter and public safety is the first priority in every fire management activity.
- The role of wildland fire as an essential ecological process and natural change agent will be incorporated into the planning process. Federal agency land and resource management plans set the objectives for the use and desired future condition of the various public lands.
- Fire management plans; programs, and activities support land and resource management plans and their implementation.

- Sound risk management is a foundation for all fire management activities. Risks and uncertainties relating to fire management activities must be understood, analyzed, communicated, and managed as they relate to the cost of either doing or not doing an activity. Net gains to the public benefit will be an important component of decisions.
- Fire management program and activities are economically viable, based upon values to be protected, costs, and land and resource management objectives. Federal agency administrators are adjusting and reorganizing programs to reduce costs and increase efficiencies. As part of this process, investments in fire management activities must be evaluated against other agency programs in order to effectively accomplish the overall mission, set short- and long-term priorities, and clarify management accountability.
- Fire management plans and activities-are based upon the best available science. Knowledge and experience are developed among all wildland fire management agencies. An active fire research program combined with interagency collaboration provides the means to make this available to all fire managers.
- Fire management plans and activities incorporate public health and environmental quality considerations.
- Federal, State, Tribal, and local interagency coordination and cooperation are essential. Increasing costs and smaller work forces require that public agencies pool their human resources to successfully deal with the ever-increasing and more complex fire management tasks. Full collaboration among Federal agencies and between the Federal agencies and State, local, and private entities results in a mobile fire management work force available to the full range of public needs.
- Standardization of policies and procedures among Federal agencies is an ongoing objective. Consistency of plans and operations provides the fundamental platform upon which Federal agencies can cooperate and integrate fire activities across agency boundaries and provide leadership for cooperation with State and local fire management organizations.
- Good data and statistics are needed to support fire management decisions. Agencies must jointly establish an accurate, compatible, and accessible database of fire- and ecosystem-related data.

The 2009 fire policy document continued, expanded, and clarified the 1995 guiding principles.

- *National Strategic Planning:* National level strategic planning for wildland fire management has been intensively pursued over recent years. The National Cohesive Wildland Fire Management Strategy, completed in April 2014, http://www.forestsandrangelands.gov/strategy/), accomplishes several important tasks. It establishes a national vision for wildland fire management, defines three national goals, describes the wildland fire challenges, identifies opportunities to reduce wildfire risks, and establishes national priorities focused on achieving the national goals.
  The Cohesive Strategy recognizes and accepts fire as a natural process necessary for the maintenance of many ecosystems, and endeavors to reduce conflicts between fire-prone landscapes and people. By considering the role of fire in the landscape, the ability of humans to plan for and adapt to living with fire, and the need to be prepared to respond to fire when it occurs, the Cohesive Strategy takes a holistic approach to the future of wildland fire management.
  The Cohesive Strategy presents a vision adopted by the Wildland Fire Leadership Council (WFLC) for the next century: *To safely and effectively extinguish fire, when needed; use fire where allowable; manage our natural resources; and as a Nation, live with wildland fire.*

To achieve this vision, the Cohesive Strategy identifies the necessary goals identified to be:

- Restore and maintain landscapes:
- Landscapes across all jurisdictions are resilient to fire related disturbances in accordance with management objectives.
- Fire-adapted communities: Human populations and infrastructure can withstand a wildfire without loss of life and property.
- Wildfire response: All jurisdictions participate in making and implementing safe, effective, efficient risk-based wildfire management decisions.

Early in the planning process, stakeholders collaboratively established the following guiding principles and core values for wildland fire management to guide fire and land management activities:

- Reducing risk to firefighters and the public is the first priority in every fire management activity.
- Sound risk management is the foundation for all management activities.
- Actively manage the land to make it more resilient to disturbance, in accordance with management objectives.
- Improve and sustain both community and individual responsibilities to prepare for, respond to, and recover from wildfire through capacity-building activities.
- Rigorous wildfire prevention programs are supported across all jurisdictions.
- Wildland fire, as an essential ecological process and natural change agent, may be incorporated into the planning process and wildfire response.
- Fire management decisions are based on the best available science, knowledge, and experience, and used to evaluate risk versus gain.
- Local, state, tribal, and Federal agencies support one another with wildfire response, including engagement in collaborative planning and the decision-making processes that take into account all lands and recognize the interdependence and statutory responsibilities among jurisdictions.
- Where land and resource management objectives differ, prudent and safe actions must be taken through collaborative fire planning and suppression response to keep unwanted wildfires from spreading to adjacent jurisdictions.
- Safe aggressive initial attack is often the best suppression strategy to keep unwanted wildfires small and costs down.
- Fire management programs and activities are economically viable and commensurate with values to be protected, land and resource management objectives, and social and environmental quality considerations.
- National Wildland Fire Management Program Review and Strategic Risk Assessment: The 2014 Quadrennial Fire Review (QFR) (http://forestsandrangelands.gov/QFR/reports.shtml) Is the third iteration of a

> strategic risk assessment process initiated by the United States Department of Agriculture (USDA) and the Department of the Interior (DOI). It is a joint effort of the USDA Forest Service Fire & Aviation Management (FS-FAM) and the DOI Office of Wildland Fire (OWF), which coordinates the wildland fire management efforts of four DOI bureaus: the Bureau of Land Management (BLM), the National Park Service (NPS), the US Fish and Wildlife Service (FWS), and the Bureau of Indian Affairs (BIA).

The 2014 QFR sought to identify and explore key wildland fire management issues in the United States; assess the efficacy of current policy, strategy, and programs in expected future environments; and present a set of related actions for consideration by federal wildland fire leaders at the FS and the DOI. A future-oriented mindset was integral to the process; a central aim of the QFR was to offer wildland fire leaders the opportunity to methodically analyze a set of alternative futures that could emerge over the next 10 to 20 years. The QFR links closely with the National Cohesive Wildland Fire Management Strategy Cohesive Strategy process. Whereas the Cohesive Strategy assesses the current situation and outlines actions to improve near-term effectiveness, the QFR looks 10 to 20 years forward to explore a range of plausible alternative futures, offers an analytical underpinning for the next Cohesive Strategy, and encourages present-day preparation for emerging change. The 2014 QFR process included a "baseline assessment" focused on four key issue areas (changing climatic conditions, risk management, workforce, and operational capabilities), development of four plausible alternative futures set in 2034 and related insights, and distillation of eight strategic-level conclusions and actions for consideration by fire leaders.

The current fire policy is far and away the most comprehensive and applicable policy fire management has ever had. The National Cohesive Strategy represents the single best strategic assessment completed for fire management, corresponds closely with the federal fire policy, and frames program needs perfectly described for this transformative time in program the fire environment evolution. The QFR provides a strategic look at program trajectory and offers a longer-term viewpoint framed in several different options. Several key commonalities are found in these framework documents. The importance of these areas is reflected in their continued presence in guiding documents. They all speak to safety of firefighters and the public; sound risk management, the importance of science, a need to restore and maintain landscapes, and improving wildfire response.

Risk Management: Risk management is emerging as a prominent wildland fire management subject. The Federal Fire Policy and the National Cohesive Wildland Fire Management Strategy emphasize the value of risk management, and the US Forest Service has made clear its goal to become a risk management organization. Land and fire managers are increasingly asked to adopt risk management principles, to analyze and communicate risks, and to make risk-informed decisions. In addition, an improved understanding of human behavior - at individual, group and organizational levels – is vital to making fire management safer, more active, progressive, and adaptable. These are far-reaching topical areas that include, but are not limited to, firefighter and public safety, best practices in safety training and operations, safety related research, new approaches to safety, fire response, safety issues in wildland urban interfaces, training, equipment and technology, risk assessment, risk informed decision-making, high reliability organizations, sense-making, shared responsibility, preparedness, organizational discipline, organizational performance, organizational breakdown, decision making, communications, resilience, risk, decision support, community and homeowner fire protection and hazard mitigation, fire education, and social, economic, and political effects of fires.

The United States Forest Service, the largest wildland fire management organization in the United States, is progressively expanding its perspective that development and implementation of strategies to manage wildland fire that avoid ecosystem degradation and better account for firefighter and public safety in both the short term and the long term are critically important. Wildland fire management has expanded from a limited tactical and physical perspective to a more all-inclusive approach that includes attention to risk management, human dimensions, and decision making that support and improve organizational performance, safety, and accomplishment of social, political, and ecological objectives.

Risk is not only associated with the human factors but also with ecological concerns. Many wildland ecosystems are at risk of damaging wildfire, invasive species, habitat fragmentation, and other disturbance agents. The long-term risk of short-term inaction is high and mitigation is necessary in the form of fuel treatment, vegetation management, prescribed fire, and the use of wildland fire.

Risk assessment tools useful for decision support are increasing. Science and technology products are emerging at much faster rates than ever before and incorporation of new tools is rapidly expanding management capabilities. The 2009 federal fire policy implementation guidance recommended the incorporation of science and technology and specifically advocated for advanced decision support products. One such product, the Wildland Fire Decision Support System, has been adopted and used for decision support and documentation on thousands of fires (see attached briefing paper).

AUGUST 25, 2015

Wildland Fire Decision Support System (WFDSS)

Background

The Wildland Fire Decision Support System (WFDSS) system was developed to assist line officers, fire managers and analysts in managing wildland fire incidents. It is intended to streamline and improve wildland fire decision-making.

WFDSS supports risk-informed decision-making by providing access to data and incorporating improvements in technology, fire modeling capability, and geospatial analysis into a web based scalable system. This system provides a location to document decisions, supports analysis, and facilitates completion of operational plans. It utilizes fire behavior modeling, fire weather information, economic principles, and information technology to support effective wildland fire decisions consistent with Land and Resource Management Plans and Fire Management Plans.

Advantages of WFDSS over previous systems include:

- Use of fire management strategic objectives from land, resource, and fire management plans and intelligence such as fuel conditions, fire danger and weather analysis, fire history, fire behavior projections, probability of fire reaching a point of interest, inventory of values to be protected, stratified cost index, relative risk and organization assessment.
- It is linear, scalable, progressive, and responsive to fire complexity.
- It is spatially oriented, graphically displayed, with no reliance on large text input requirements.

Characteristics of WFDSS

- Managers begin the decision process at fire discovery.

- Managers can view land management objectives tied to geospatial references and utilize risk assessment outputs accessible to all interested parties through a web-based system.
- Risk assessment information includes weather data and forecasts, fire danger information, fire behavior predictive and smoke modeling tools, economic assessments, relative risk rating, and landscape value inventories.
- A wide variety of spatial information products and models have been integrated into WFDSS with a map based user interface, and include:
    - LANDFIRE spatial fuels data,
    - National Weather Service forecasts and outlooks, along with climate and fire danger from the Weather Information Management System,
    - USGS and Google Map products,
    - Fire Spread Probability (FSPro) spread simulation probability and fire behavior products
    - Basic, Short Term, and Near Term fire behavior models
    - Stratified Cost Index (SCI)
    - Values Information & Values at Risk products,
    - Natural resource management spatial themes,
    - Local unit spatial fire planning spatial data,
    - Estimated ground evacuation spatial data.

Development for FY2015 incorporated input from a user centered design review that resulted in an intuitive simple decision editor. There was also security maintenance, hardware migrations and continued focus on system reliability relating to spatial and data aspects which made the application more robust.

Although future improvements to the system are uncertain, routine maintenance and system reliability fixes will take place over time. Potential development includes increased information for use in risk assessment and firefighter exposure determinations, updates to the fire behavior models, and automation of reporting requirements. These improvements are not all-inclusive or approved but are being considered at this time.

Use of WFDSS

Since WFDSS delivery in April of 2009 there have been 90,763 wildland fire incidents entered into the system while calendar year 2015 has seen 14,792 incidents entered as of August 25, 2015. All five Federal wildland fire management agencies, State organizations, Tribes, and Alaska Native Corporations are represented in these figures. WFDSS is now integrated with iRWIn (Integrated Reporting of Wildland-Fire Information). WFDSS sends and receives data through iRWIn, reducing duplicative data entry for field users. Sharing data amongst fire applications is improving the accuracy and quality of the data.

Management Implications

This decision support system increases access to information which leads to improved science based and risk informed decision-making. It presents a consistent decision documentation and analysis system that allows managers of all agencies to work through an identical process, it is useful across jurisdictional boundaries, and is supportive of individual agency objectives and needs. Its scalability and flexibility allows decision documentation, planning, and analysis activities to match incident complexity and duration. These features may improve natural and community resource protection, management response effectiveness, use of firefighting resources, and potentially reduce firefighter exposure and suppression costs.

WEBSITES FOR ADDITIONAL INFORMATION

WFM RD&A Website – www.wfmrda.nwcg.gov
WFDSS Website – https://wfdss.usgs.gov
WFDSS Overview - http://wfdss.usgs.gov/wfdss/pdfs/wfdss overview%2002 02 15.pdf

Budget

The IAWF enthusiastically surges the Committee to work across party lines to reform how the nation budgets for wildfires. Each year continues to bear out that complexity of the social, political and ecological factors influencing the fire environment, fire planning, and operational activities is increasing. To meet the requirements and needs of all of these elements, it is bluntly obvious that the cost of business is increasing. As fire managers in the field face the complexities of managing wildland fire, the Department of the Interior and U.S. Forest Service continue to struggle with the existing budget process used by Congress to fund fire suppression activities. Currently, the budget for wildland fire uses a ten-year average of fire suppression costs. In a peak fire season with catastrophic fires, if the available suppression funding falls short, the agencies are forced to move funds from other programs ("fire borrowing") to meet the increased wildfire suppression costs. This undermines other important programs, including critically important forest and rangeland management and fire risk reduction activities.

We support a budget process that will solve the fire budget problem and provide additional capacity for the agencies to invest in forest and rangeland restoration making landscapes less vulnerable and more resilient to fire. We have actively supported earlier efforts for wildfire disaster funding and believe that such funding should initiate before 100 percent of the 10-year average suppression costs are spent. This will permit more flexibility and minimize adverse impacts of fire transfers on the budgets of other fire and non-fire programs. A budget neutral process is needed that would allow natural resource management agencies to budget for wildfires in the same manner as other natural disasters.

Opportunities to enhance fuels management and restoration work make lands more resilient to fire, reduce the risks to the public and firefighters, and can support long-term reductions in suppression costs. Fire resilient lands and communities mean that both can withstand the effects of the fire without significant loss of life, property or ecosystems. Fuel treatment, vegetation management, and restoration activities remain a significant need and accomplishments must be increased.

To summarize, while we believe that much time could be devoted to advocating for budget increases, we appreciate the reality of budgetary increases. So, other ways to capitalize on opportunities to improve the organizational response of the federal agencies to the management of wildland fires must be pursued. As stated above, policy and guiding documentation is at its best level and affords the agencies strong opportunities. Agencies must be supported and allowed to implement the program within these guidelines. Risk management, as identified throughout the fire policy, National Cohesive Strategy, and QFR, should be adopted as a principal component of base fire management. Risk-based decision-making can reduce firefighter and equipment exposure, support response activities, and serve the greater good over the long-term. It was recently stated that what is viewed as the current fire problem is, in reality, a land management problem. We have long-term needs to reduce fuels, re-introduce fire into ecosystems, harden communities, strengthen response capabilities, and realize the full spectrum of opportunities afforded by the guiding framework, a risk management approach, and complementary rather than restrictive budget processes. A well-planned course can make substantial and well-needed differences in the fire situation. Short-term fixes are unlikely and long-term patience and commitment is necessary from society in order to effect needed changes.

Thank you again for this opportunity and your time today.

In: Federal Management of Wildland Fire
Editor: Rebecca Salazar
ISBN: 978-1-63484-864-0

Chapter 5

Testimony of Dr. Michael Medler, Spokesman, Firefighters United for Safety, Ethics & Ecology. Hearing on "Federal Agency Wildfire Management"*

Chairman Murkowski, ranking member Cantwell, and members of the Committee, I want to thank you for this chance to testify about our "opportunities to improve federal wildland fire management." It is a real honor to be here.

My name is Michael Medler, and I teach at Western Washington University. I am also a member of Firefighters United for Safety, Ethics and Ecology (FUSEE) and I have worked as a wildland firefighter for the U.S. Forest Service, including some very formative time fighting the massive Yellowstone fires in 1988. In the 1990s I went on to get a Ph.D. developing systems for mapping and modeling wildland fires. Since then, I have served as the president of The Association for Fire Ecology, and was the founding editor of the scientific journal *Fire Ecology*. Now, I work with students that are studying wildfire and heading back to the fire lines each summer.

This week, the people of Washington State are mourning the loss of three more wildland firefighters. My heart really goes out to their families and friends. But let me put a different personal face on all this. I have several

* This is an edited, reformatted and augmented version of testimony presented August 27, 2015 for a Seattle field hearing of the Senate Energy and Natural Resources Committee.

daughters. One of them is a 19-year-old named Bodie. She is a tall collegiate rower who can lift heavy things all day long and she is comfortable sleeping in the dirt. In short, she would be great addition to any fire crew. Since she was little, I have been suggesting that she work on fire crews during the summers in college and perhaps look at it as a career. But after the last few fire seasons, as a father, I am finding it more and more difficult to keep recommending it to her or my students.

To echo many others who have testified before this committee, and to put it bluntly, the last century of fire policies have left our forests explosive, and our fire fighters are being placed in increasingly difficult situations. Climate change is combining with years of fire suppression to create larger and hotter fires, and development has left thousands of communities vulnerable to fires that used to happen miles from anyone. To make matters worse, our wildland firefighters are trained for the backcountry, but they are increasingly trying to protect communities from these hotter fires. Meanwhile, our national firefighting costs are going up, even in our moderate years. This is all the new normal. Therefore, we cannot keep using suppression policies and fire practices from the last century.

Today I am here as a constituent of Senator Cantwell and I am also here representing FUSEE, which is a nonprofit organization dedicated to uniting wildland firefighters and other fire management professionals in support of safe, ethical, and ecological management of wildland fire. One thing that unites the people who work with FUSEE is the understanding that we don't need to sacrifice ecological or ethical standards to fight wildfire safely. In fact, I would argue that if we can find ways of living with fire in most of its natural forms, while working in concert with our communities to make them more fire resilient, we can maximize fire fighter safety and reduce the costs. However, what we need is a new paradigm and clear congressional guidance.

For example, the "Big Three" causes of large wildfires and high suppression costs are climate change, fuel accumulation, and sprawl in the Wildland Urban Interface (WUI). This trifecta will take decades to fix, but the choices that fire managers make before the fire season, and the decisions they make on each fire can have huge and immediate effects on firefighter safety, costs, and environmental impacts.

The fire landscape of the U.S. is complicated and fires burn differently in different places. Solutions for Washington State will look very different than solutions for Arizona. Nevertheless, Congress is in a position to provide the leadership to achieve real differences across private, public, national, and local interests.

I am a trained geographer. I think about things spatially. For example, in the U.S. we have about a billion burnable acres. The Forest Service estimates that we need active management to reduce the fuel loads on nearly half of that, or about 400 million of those acres. That is an area larger than the entire state of Alaska that needs fuel reductions to improve our forest health.

At this point the Forest Service has come a long way with their fuels reduction program. However, they are still only treating about 2 million acres per year with a little over a half-million acres treated mechanically and the rest with fire. Unfortunately, this is not even approaching the rate at which we are adding new lands to the backlog needing treatment. We are already suffering from an "ecological fire deficit" of over 12 million acres each year in just the 11 conterminous western states. Therefore, to really make inroads in our treatment program we need to increase the acreage treated by roughly an order of magnitude, and even at 20 million acres a year we would still need decades to address these problems. Interestingly, this 20 million acre number is very similar to the acreage of fire we were experiencing annually in the U.S. before we developed effective fire suppression techniques in the 1940s and 1950s.

To actively treat anything like 20 millions of acres per year we will have to use fire. These sorts of numbers are simply beyond the reach of mechanical thinning. As a young man, I spent some time working in the woods doing mechanical thinning. We would work in groups of five to ten, using chainsaws and then burning the piles. It could take us several days to clear and burn the brush on a few acres. Therefore, I am quite impressed that the Forest Service is currently successfully treating as much as they are. However, this problem is vastly larger than any mechanical solution we can develop. Simply put, we can't cut our way out of this. Additionally, much of the 400 million acres that need treatment are in steep, rugged terrain that is difficult to work in. Even if we could do it, cutting and thinning is expensive to subsidize in many of these areas, it can have harsh ecological consequences, and done poorly it actually exacerbates fire hazards in the future.

Instead, we are going to need to find ways to reestablish fire's traditional ecological role on millions of acres per year, and this project is going to require a combination of prescribed fire and ecologically managed wildland fires that are much larger than we are seeing now. However, over time, in many areas, these ecological efforts will create a patchy mosaic of reduced fire hazards and reestablish historical fire regimes that will be safer and cheaper to manage.

Currently, the real problem with managing and reestablishing these sorts of large fires is that we now have about 70,000 communities, and millions of homes, at risk from wildland fire and about 200 million acres of land is now in our Wildland Urban Interface or WUI with almost 30 million of those acres in the western U.S.

But here is what is interesting. It is really the last quarter mile around our communities that is the most important. That is where you can stop a fire from burning buildings. That is where thinning, fuels management, building codes, and enhanced local firefighting capabilities can make a real difference. What is surprising is that a quarter mile buffer around every named place in the U.S. Census in the entire western U.S. makes up less than 9 million acres. That is an area more like the size of the state of Maryland. This "Community Protection Zone" is where we do have the resources to make a difference.

What we need is a "Marshal Plan" providing guidance and funding for the work that needs to be done in these areas and in the surrounding WUI. With congressional guidance, we could create good local jobs that could include fire mitigation and WUI firefighting specialists. This is the best place to work with local industry and to use biomass to offset costs. This is also the area to help organize and empower local communities.

The federal government does not hold much of the land surrounding many of these communities, and our last few big fires in Washington have been burning through a patchwork that included surprisingly little federal land. Therefore, we are going to need innovative funding and policy proposals to help improve the resilience of these communities. But the good news is that all this can be directed to a remarkably small part of our burnable landscape.

As Stephen Pyne testified before this committee several months ago, some communities need to be "hardened" to better resist wildland fire, so that we have the options of doing restoration work at the vast scale necessary in the backcountry. If people and communities are prepared and protected from fire, this expands our options and opportunities to manage wildfires in other areas of the WUI and especially deeper into the backcountry. It is around these communities that mechanical thinning combined with prescribed burning will be of the most use. Then we can really start to address the restoration of our forests and develop a new resilient system of backcountry fire management. This would include broad scale management with active fire use in ways that help restore ecosystems and reduce the likelihood of extreme fire behavior.

By prioritizing our fire mitigation efforts in the dense parts of the WUI, we can facilitate the use of fire on millions of other acres in the backcountry. Not only would this enhance ecological restoration and forest health, but it would also be vastly cheaper than trying to fight all of our largest fires. By reducing the use of aircraft and limiting the amount of direct attack by hand crews in the backcountry, we would both reduce the costs and provide for a safer work environment for our firefighters. Best of all, reintroducing fire into these landscapes would shift from being simply a one-time emergency expense and instead become an investment in future fire management. We would be using backcountry fire to reduce the long-term damage to forest health while actually providing a more resilient landscape to manage future fires while also reducing future expenditures.

These changes will require extensive policy and strategic changes. My written testimony includes an extensive set of recommendations along those lines. But key among them is the idea that ultimately, the ethical use of public resources and the ecological restoration of fire-adapted ecosystems will improve safety for firefighters and the citizens they serve while also bringing down the costs. These changes would also require the development of new career paths in the fire community. For example, front country mitigation work in the WUI could be year round work for professionals that could also be trained in the complicated intersection of urban and wildland firefighting that occurs in the WUI. Alternatively, other members of the community could specialize in the backcountry fire use and fire monitoring skills that would allow a few dozen professionals to manage backcountry fires that now require thousands of fire fighters and millions of dollars.

I know better than most that there is no way to eliminate all the danger in this business. We can't stop all the fires. We can't protect every home in the woods, and we can't make fire fighting a totally safe profession. However, we owe it to the people living in our forests and grasslands to do what we can to protect their communities, and we owe it to all the people we put on the fire lines to do all we can to keep them safer while still managing our landscapes in ways that allow fire to be the natural process it is.

I really want to be able to keep recommending a career in wildland fire to my students and especially to my daughters.

Thank you for time.

Below are additional key points and recommendations from FUSEE for Congressional support to help shift the paradigm of federal wildland fire management, organized by key topics.

Community Fire Preparation

- If communities and homes are prepared and protected from fire damage, this expands options and opportunities to manage wildfires in backcountry wildlands. Firefighters need a partnership with homeowners, rural residents, and private property owners to prepare for wildland fire of all kinds: prescribed fire, wildland fire use, and wildfire suppression. Some homes have been destroyed by escaped prescribed fires, and many opportunities to manage backcountry wildfires for resource and ecosystem benefits have been missed because of the risk of wildfire spreading to unprepared homes and communities. The sooner we prepare communities and homes for fire, the sooner we can restore backcountry wildlands with fire.
- We need resources and education to facilitate a program of "prepare, leave early, or stay and defend" instead of mass evacuations that empty communities of the labor force needed to protect structures. It is typically not a "tsunami" of flame that destroys structures, but tiny embers that land on rooftops, or surface fires creeping through pine needles on the ground, and trained volunteers and residents watching out over their own property could stop these. Firefighters cannot provide structure protection for every house since a single wildfire could simultaneously put hundreds of homes at risk. Homeowners and residents who have prepared their homes to be fire-resistant should be supported with technical assistance, training, and resources to help protect their own homes. This may enable wildland firefighters to better focus on what they are trained and equipped to do—wildland fire management—rather than structural fire protection.
- We should consider mobilizing more community volunteers to help prepare communities for wildfire well before fires, by reducing flammable vegetation and combustible fuels (e.g. firewood piles) within the Home Ignition Zone, a relatively narrow band around structures that is the most critical terrain in terms of preventing wildfires from igniting structures. There are also ample opportunities for small businesses to help retrofit structures with non-flammable materials, such as metal roofs, that also greatly improve the probability of structures withstanding wildfire events. Much of the work of community fire preparation is labor-intensive, and opportunity exists to tap into civic-minded community groups and

volunteer organizations, especially providing opportunities for young people to do the hard physical labor of mitigating fuel hazards and fire risks on private property in rural communities.

- We must consider raising some "taboo" subjects in western communities, such as zoning laws that prohibit new home construction in indefensible locations of undeveloped wildlands, vegetation management ordinances that prevent excessive build-up of hazardous fuels on private lands, building codes to require fire-resistant designs and materials used in construction, and community fire planning needed to live sustainably in fire-prone landscapes. While respecting private property rights, policymakers should do more to encourage community responsibilities needed by developers, homeowners, and other rural residents to prevent home losses from wildfire.

Suppression Costs versus Fuels Reduction and Forest Restoration Investments

- We should beware of using emergency accounts like FEMA disaster recovery funds to pay for wildfire suppression actions—those funds will be needed for recovery from major disasters such as earthquakes, floods, hurricanes, and tornadoes. The Pacific Northwest, for example, will experience a major earthquake disaster that may require billions of dollars for recovery, and these funds should not be siphoned off to pay for suppression actions that are separate and different from post-disaster recovery actions.
- The existing fire budget is divided into "fire preparedness" and "fire operations," but these have been wrongly defined by agencies as fire "prevention" and "suppression" at the expense of other fire management strategies. Fire operations should also include the *use* of fire (i.e. controlled burning with prescribed fires or managed wildfires). If fire use is implemented to reduce fuels or restore ecological integrity and ecosystem resilience, then expenditures for fire operations can be seen more as *investments* yielding long-term benefits rather than pure costs. Earmarking a budget for suppression-only will likely not reduce costs, and lead agencies away from fire operations that manage wildfires for resource benefits.

- The suppression budget needs to be fixed to avoid the perverse incentives caused by Congressional "blank check" funding for suppression. While budgets for fuels reduction, fire planning, fire research, and forest restoration projects that come from normal appropriations are continually getting cut, agencies essentially get rewarded for failing to do proper fire planning, or completed fuels reduction projects with near-unlimited supplemental appropriations for emergency wildfire suppression. Adequate funds must be appropriated to plan for and manage wildfire rather than just suppress it.
- Severe fire weather conditions typically shift among regions from year to year. We need to shift the focus of "severity funding" so that we pre-position extra resources not just in the regions where fire severity is predicted to be high, but also where it is predicted to be low. In regions where climate and weather conditions are conducive to low-intensity wildfire, the extra crews and resources available can allow agencies to safely apply fire use on a landscape scale. Recently burned areas are the best protection against uncharacteristic high-intensity wildfires.
- We need to track, monitor, and analyze the effects and effectiveness of air tankers before we embark on a massive investment of taxpayer dollars in a new air fleet. Important research being conducted by the Forest Service's Fire Lab in Missoula are raising critical questions about air tanker and retardant use. Retardant does not extinguish flames, it simply slows fire spread, but if ground crews are not positioned to take advantage of slowed fire spread, the effects of retardant quickly dissipate and wildfire continues to spread unchecked. From initial data, it appears that the majority of air tanker retardant drops occur in the times, places, and conditions where they are least effective. Aviation resources and retardant are typically one of the highest cost centers of suppression operations, and we need to ensure that these expenditures are worth their price. Significant numbers of fire crews could be hired for the same price we pay for air tankers and retardant, and these crews are far more versatile in performing many different fire management tasks and missions than are air tankers that have only one purpose or mission.
- We need to systematically analyze the effects of large-scale burnout or "box and burn" strategies that are becoming more prevalent in wildfire suppression, especially on large fires or during severe

weather conditions. Indirect attack with suppression firing operations may yield benefits in terms of enhanced firefighter safety as well as reintroducing fire to areas impacted from past fire exclusion, however, ecologically-appropriate fire effects must be the goal of firing operations, not just wildfire containment at the expense, and often sacrifice, of resource values and ecosystem integrity.

- We will be unable to "treat" fuels in a sufficient time and scale and acceptable cost to avoid large-scale, high-severity wildfires—wildfire itself can be the treatment for landscapes degraded by past fire exclusion. Agencies have fairly advanced technology for monitoring, mapping, and modeling fire spread and predicting fire effects, but this technology is under-utilized when firefighters are ordered to do aggressive initial attack to put fires out when they are small. Putting small fires out merely puts off big fires that will ignite in the future, likely during weather and in fuel conditions more severe due to unfolding climate change and accumulating hazardous fuel loads. Given that wildfire is a vital ecological process, and future climate and weather conditions more conducive to large wildfires are unavoidable, it is essential that agencies reintroduce fire to fire-adapted landscapes as much and as soon as is viable. The future direction for agencies is thus to manage wildfires as if they were prescribed fires, relying on careful pre-fire planning, advanced technology, and highly-skilled fire crews trained in fire use to maximize the social and ecological benefits of fire while mitigating potential adverse impacts or damages to human assets.

Firefighter and Public Safety

- There is no such thing as safe firefighting—it has inherent health hazards and safety risks, but these risks and hazards can be mitigated with careful planning, training, communications, and adequate resources. We need to ensure that firefighters are not needlessly exposed to hazards and risks, so we must be more selective and strategic in the places and conditions we suppress wildfire, and shift from reactively suppressing nearly all wildfires in a state of emergency and crisis-management mode, to proactively managing and utilizing most wildfires to maximize the socioeconomic, natural resource, and ecosystem benefits of fire. In short, we need to stop "blindly" fighting all fires and start wisely managing every fire.

- We must shift to a more rational, rules-based system for dispatching crews based on risk assessment rather than "knee-jerk" aggressive initial attack suppression responses immediately after fire detection. We need to abandon the paradox of mandating aggressive initial attack on all fires during conditions of severe fire weather or suppression resource shortage—our firefighting efforts are largely futile and not worth the risk to firefighters.
- There are "externalized" long-term risks to firefighters and communities from continued focus on short-term suppression and fire exclusion that defers wildfires to future, when we are likely to experience even more severe fuel and weather conditions because of climate change. Risk assessments must incorporate both short-term and long-term risks, and include potential social and ecological benefits of fire.
- Ultimately, ethical use of public resources and ecological restoration of fire-adapted ecosystems will make it safer for firefighters and the citizens they serve. Simply adding more taxpayer money or resources without ensuring that they are efficiently and effectively used, or fighting fires more aggressively while ignoring the adverse environmental and ecological impacts of suppression actions, will not make it safer for firefighters or the public.

FIRE ECOLOGY, MANAGEMENT AND TREATMENTS

- We need to both recover from the historical ecological fire deficit, reduce fuels, restore ecosystems altered by past fire exclusion, and prepare landscapes for increased wildfire activity and large wildfires given climate change. Large wildfires pose both potential risks and benefits, and we need to consider both in strategic wildfire management that utilizes the best fire ecology science and advanced technology for monitoring, mapping, and modeling wildfires to utilize more wildfire ignitions for fuels reduction and ecosystem restoration objectives. Thus, fire managers and firefighters need training in ecological fire management and fire use.

- We need to fully implement the Federal Wildland Fire Management Policy as the foundational philosophy for fire management on federal lands. The Federal fire policy states that it is the current and expected condition of the fire, not its source or location, that should determine the management response. We should never again allow national decrees against fire use to be issued from the Washington Office of the Forest Service, nor should Regional Foresters issue similar directives that declare total suppression of all wildfires including those located in remote backcountry wildlands or designated wilderness areas.
- Prescribed burning faces numerous social, legal, and fiscal constraints that limit its scope. Therefore, wildfire management or "fire use" is the most natural, most practical, and most economical way to both reduce fuels and restore ecosystems at the scale necessary. When and where conditions permit, plans exist, and resources are available, wildfires should be managed with the same principles, goals and objectives as prescribed fires. Different from "let it burn," wildfires should be actively managed to achieve desired fire behavior and fire effects.
- Strategically placed fuels treatments, rather than landscape-wide mechanical treatments, can have the greatest impact on fire spread and effects at a much lower cost. Fuels treatments must be oriented to safe reintroduction of fire and ecological use of wildfire, not continued fire suppression and exclusion.
- We need to invest in spatial fire management planning so we can opportunistically manage wildfires with prescribed fire principles for community protection and ecosystem restoration objectives. Spatial fire planning should be used to identify natural "firesheds" where wildfire can burn within natural barriers or confines.

In: Federal Management of Wildland Fire ISBN: 978-1-63484-864-0
Editor: Rebecca Salazar

Chapter 6

GUIDANCE FOR IMPLEMENTATION OF FEDERAL WILDLAND FIRE MANAGEMENT POLICY*

Fire Executive Council

FOREWORD

The Review and Update of the 1995 Federal Wildland Fire Management Policy (January 2001) is the primary interagency wildland fire policy document. The Interagency Strategy for the Implementation of Federal Wildland Fire Management Policy (June 20, 2003) was developed and approved under the authority of the Wildland Fire Leadership Council (WFLC) to set forth direction for consistent implementation of the federal fire policy. It has been used since that time.

On May 2, 2008, the WFLC issued a memorandum entitled Modification of Federal Wildland Fire Policy Guidance. This memorandum directed federal agencies to test and implement new guidelines for wildland fire management. The modifications were tested in a number of field units in the 2008 fire season.

In 2009 the National Wildfire Coordinating Group (NWCG) issued a memorandum to the NWCG executive board (NWCG#001-2009, January 7,

* This is an edited, reformatted and augmented version of an interagency document dated February 13, 2009 and issued by the National Interagency Fire Center.

2009) that 1) affirms the soundness of the Review and Update of the 1995 Federal Wildland Fire Management Policy (January 2001), 2) reiterates the policy changes stated in the May 2, 2008 WFLC memorandum entitled Modification of Federal Wildland Fire Policy Guidance, 3) states that the Wildland Fire Decision Support System (WFDSS) will replace existing analysis and decision processes, and 4) confirms that the Interagency Strategy for the Implementation of Federal Wildland Fire Management Policy (June 20, 2003) will be replaced in 2009.

This document, Guidance for Implementation of Federal Wildland Fire Management Policy (February, 2009), is that replacement.

FIRE EXECUTIVE COUNCIL

February 13, 2009 Memorandum

To:	Chief, USDA Forest Service
	Director, Bureau of Indian Affairs
	Director, Bureau of Land Management
	Director, Fish and Wildlife Service
	Director, National Park Service
From:	Chair, Fire Executive Council
Subject:	Guidance for Implementation of Federal Wildland Fire Policy

On February 13, 2009, the Fire Executive Council (FEC) approved Guidance for the Implementation of Federal Wildland Fire Management Policy. This Guidance provides for consistent implementation of the 1995/2001 Federal Fire Policy, as directed by the Wildland Fire Leadership Council.

Successful implementation of the Guidance requires that each of the federal wildland fire agencies work together through development of unified direction and guidance for agency/bureau manuals, directives, handbooks, guidebooks, plans agreements and other pertinent documents to complete final implementation of this guidance.

In approving the Guidance the FEC:

- directs the National Wildfire Coordinating Group to adopt the guidance and review and revise, as appropriate, all interagency training courses, operational guides, standards, terminology, reporting requirements skill/competency/qualification/certification requirements and other pertinent documents.

- directs the federal fire directors to work collaboratively with state, local and tribal fire managers and public and nongovernment organizations to communicate direction stated in the guidance with internal and external audiences to foster understanding and support for the complexity of wildland fire management.
- directs the federal fire directors to revise or develop accountability standards, performance measures and tracking systems to assess if resource and protection objectives are met during the course of management on all wildland fires.

We thank the interagency team that produced this implementation guidance and extend special appreciation to the National Association of State Forest, International Association of Fire Chiefs, National Association of Counties, The Wilderness Society, and The Nature Conservancy for the support and commitment in completing the document.

APPROVAL

The *Guidance for Implementation of the Federal Wildland Fire Policy (February, 2009)* is hereby approved by the Fire Executive Council. Implementation actions are to begin immediately.

U.S. Department of Agriculture Date
Forest Service, Fire & Aviation Management
Tom Harbour, Director

Department of the Interior Date
Office of Wildland Fire Coordination
Kirk Rowdabaugh, Director

Bureau of Land Management Date
Fire and Aviation Management Directorate
Jim Douglas, Assistant Director

National Park Service Date
Visitor and Resource Protection
Karen Taylor-Goodrich, Associate Director

Fish and Wildlife Service Date
National Wildlife Refuge System
Division Natural Resource and Conservation Planning
Andy Loranger, Chief

Bureau of Indian Affairs Date
Trust Services
Vicki Forrest, Deputy Director

Department of the Interior National Business Center – Aviation Management Directorate Mark Bathrick, Associate Director	Date	National Wildfire Coordinating Group Ex officio Brian McManus, Chair	Date

INTRODUCTION

The *Review and Update of the 1995 Federal Wildland Fire Management Policy (January 2001)* remains sound and presents a single cohesive federal fire policy for the Departments of the Interior and Agriculture. However, some issues associated with implementation of this policy need closer attention and clarification to fully achieve the intent of the policy.

One such policy area is the Wildland Urban Interface (WUI). WUI is more complex and extensive than previously considered in the 1995 and 2001 Federal Fire Policy reviews. Fire management activities affecting WUI areas require closer coordination and more engagement between with federal, state, local and tribal land and fire managers to ensure firefighter and public safety and mitigate property loss from wildland fire.

A key finding of the 2001 review of the 1995 policy was that "multiple terms for various management options to respond to wildland fire have confused agency managers and employees, operators, partners, and the public, and have perpetuated multiple fire management program elements". This important communications issue will be resolved only through federal, state, local and tribal engagement in building a foundation for common terms (see Appendix A) with understanding and support by all.

The current policy clearly states that wildland fire analysis will carefully consider the long-term benefits in relation to risks both in the short and long term:

> "Fire, as a critical natural process, will be integrated into land and resource management plans and activities on a landscape scale, and across agency boundaries. Response to wildland fire is based on ecological, social, and legal consequences of fire. The circumstances under which a fire occurs, and the likely consequences on firefighter and public safety and welfare, natural and cultural resources, and values to be protected dictate the appropriate management response to fire."

1995/2001 Federal Wildland Fire Management Policy

The intent of this framework is to solidify that the full range of strategic and tactical options are available and considered in the response to every wildland fire. These options are to be used to achieve objectives as described in Land and Resource Management Plans and/or Fire Management Plans, subject to clear processes defined to manage fire that crosses jurisdictional boundaries. Mutually developed objectives with adjoining jurisdictions for managing fires that crosses jurisdictional boundaries will also be recognized.

This guidance also calls for increased dialogue and collaboration between federal agencies and tribal, local, and state agencies as plans are updated and implemented to manage wildfires in order to accomplish resource and protection objectives.

This document, *Guidance for Implementation of Federal Wildland Fire Management Policy (February 2009)*, replaces the *Interagency Strategy for the Implementation of Federal Wildland Fire Management Policy (June 20, 2003).* This updated guidance consolidates and clarifies changes that have occurred since the 2003 strategy document was issued, and provides revised direction for consistent implementation of the *Review and Update of the 1995 Federal Wildland Fire Management Policy (January 2001)*

GUIDANCE FOR IMPLEMENTATION

The following guidelines should be used to provide consistent implementation of federal wildland fire policy. Further guidance is provided in the Federal Wildland Fire Management Policy section Table 1.

1) Wildland fire management agencies will use common standards for all aspects of their fire management programs to facilitate effective collaboration among cooperating agencies.
2) Agencies and bureaus will review, update, and develop agreements that clarify the jurisdictional inter-relationships and define the roles and responsibilities among local, state, tribal and federal fire protection entities.
3) Responses to wildland fire will be coordinated across levels of government regardless of the jurisdiction at the ignition source.
4) Fire management planning will be intergovernmental in scope and developed on a landscape scale.

5) Wildland fire is a general term describing any non-structure fire that occurs in the wildland. Wildland fires are categorized into two distinct types:
   a) Wildfires – Unplanned ignitions or prescribed fires that are declared wildfires
   b) Prescribed Fires - Planned ignitions.
6) A wildland fire may be concurrently managed for one or more objectives and objectives can change as the fire spreads across the landscape. Objectives are affected by changes in fuels, weather, topography; varying social understanding and tolerance; and involvement of other governmental jurisdictions having different missions and objectives.
7) Management response to a wildland fire on federal land is based on objectives established in the applicable Land/ Resource Management Plan and/or the Fire Management Plan.
8) Initial action on human-caused wildfire will be to suppress the fire at the lowest cost with the fewest negative consequences with respect to firefighter and public safety.
9) Managers will use a decision support process to guide and document wildfire management decisions. The process will provide situational assessment, analyze hazards and risk, define implementation actions, and document decisions and rationale for those decisions.

IMPLEMENTATION

Each of the departments or agencies participating in the review will adopt the *Guidance for Implementation of Federal Wildland Fire Management Policy (February 2009)* and review and revise, as appropriate, all manuals, handbooks, guidebooks, plans, agreements and other pertinent documents.

The National Wildfire Coordinating Group (NWCG) will adopt the *Guidance for Implementation of Federal Wildland Fire Management Policy (February 2009)* and review and revise, as appropriate, all interagency training courses, operational guides, standards, terminology, reporting requirements, skill/competency/qualification/certification requirements and other pertinent documents.

The federal fire directors, in collaboration with state, local and tribal fire managers and public and nongovernment organizations, will communicate direction stated in the *Guidance for Implementation of Federal Wildland Fire*

Management Policy (February 2009) with internal and external audiences to foster understanding and support for the complexity of wildland fire management.

The federal fire directors will revise or develop accountability standards, performance measures and tracking systems to assess if resource and protection objectives are met during the course of management on all wildland fires.

FEDERAL WILDLAND FIRE POLICY - GUIDING PRINCIPLES AND POLICY STATEMENTS

The following guiding principles and policy statements are excerpted from the *Review and Update of the 1995 Federal Wildland Fire Management Policy (January 2001).* These remain the foundational principles for Federal Wildland Fire Management Policy.

Guiding Principles

1) Firefighter and public safety is the first priority in every fire management activity.
2) The role of wildland fire as an essential ecological process and natural change agent will be incorporated into the planning process. Federal agency land and resource management plans set the objectives for the use and desired future condition of the various public lands.
3) Fire Management Plans, programs, and activities support land and resource management plans and their implementation.
4) Sound risk management is a foundation for all fire management activities. Risks and uncertainties relating to fire management activities must be understood, analyzed, communicated, and managed as they relate to the cost of either doing or not doing an activity. Net gains to the public benefit will be an important component of decisions.
5) Fire management programs and activities are economically viable, based upon values to be protected, costs, and land and resource management objectives. Federal agency administrators are adjusting and reorganizing programs to reduce costs and increase efficiencies.

As part of this process, investments in fire management activities must be evaluated against other agency programs in order to effectively accomplish the overall mission, set short- and long-term priorities, and clarify management accountability.

6) Fire Management Plans and activities are based upon the best available science. Knowledge and experience are developed among all federal wildland fire management agencies. An active fire research program combined with interagency collaboration provides the means to make these tools available to all fire managers.
7) Fire Management Plans and activities incorporate public health and environmental quality considerations.
8) Federal, State, tribal, local, interagency, and international coordination and cooperation are essential. Increasing costs and smaller work forces require that public agencies pool their human resources to successfully deal with the ever-increasing and more complex fire management tasks. Full collaboration among federal wildland fire management agencies and between the federal wildland fire management agencies and international, State, tribal, and local governments and private entities result in a mobile fire management work force available for the full range of public needs.
9) Standardization of policies and procedures among federal wildland fire management agencies is an ongoing objective. Consistency of plans and operations provides the fundamental platform upon which federal wildland fire management agencies can cooperate, integrate fire activities across agency boundaries, and provide leadership for cooperation with State, tribal, and local fire management organizations.

Federal Wildland Fire Management Policy

Each of the seventeen policy areas are assessed in depth in the following table (Table 1). The policy area's guiding principle is restated first. The left column provides statements to help clarify the Management Intent of the policy statement. The right column specifies actions needed to implement the policy statement.

Table 1. Policy Clarification of Management Intent and Implementation Actions

Policy Statement	
Management Intent	Implementation Actions
1 Safety Firefighter and public safety is the first priority. All Fire Management Plans and activities must reflect this commitment.	
No natural or cultural resource, home, or item of property is worth a human life. All strategies and tactics should seek to mitigate the risk to firefighters and the public.	Agency administrators will develop and establish process, procedures and objectives that ensure firefighter and public safety. Incident Commanders will develop and establish incident objectives, strategies and operational tactics that ensure firefighter and public safety.
2 Fire Management and Ecosystem Sustainability The full range of fire management activities will be used to help achieve ecosystem sustainability, including its interrelated ecological, economic, and social components.	
"Full range of fire management activities" may include any vegetative management treatment tool. Ecosystem sustainability provides a supply of goods, services, social values, and natural processes in perpetuity. Economic intent is to provide for sustainable supplies of goods, services, and social values through implementation of appropriate fire management activities.	Land/Resource Management Plan's (L/RMP) will be developed consistent with both ecological conditions, and fire regime dynamics, and consider the short and long term effects of both action and no action alternatives for planned vegetation management activities as well as responses to wildfire. Agencies will exploit the full range of fire management options to sustain healthy ecosystems within acceptable risk levels as identified in the L/RMP, or Fire Management Plan (FMP). Fire management activities will be based on planning and decision analysis processes that address current and anticipated situational conditions.

Table 1. (Continued)

Policy Statement	
Management Intent	Implementation Actions
3 Response to Wildland Fire Fire, as a critical natural process, will be integrated into land and resource management plans and activities on a landscape scale, and across agency boundaries. Response to wildland fires is based on ecological, social and legal consequences of the fire. The circumstances under which a fire occurs, and the likely consequences on firefighter and public safety and welfare, natural and cultural resources, and, values to be protected, dictate the appropriate response to the fire.	
The L/RMP will define and identify fire's role in the ecosystem. The response to an ignition is guided by the strategies and objectives outlined in the L/RMP and/or the Fire Management Plan. Values to be protected from and/or enhanced by wildland fire are defined in the L/RMP and/or the Fire Management Plan. L/RMP and fire management planning is coordinated across jurisdictional boundaries.	FMP's assist in developing the management response to meet L/RMP objectives in designated Fire Management Units (FMU). Fire management strategies will consider current landscape conditions and spatial and temporal components of the fire regime. Responses to wildland fires will be coordinated across jurisdictional boundaries.
4 Use of Wildland Fire Wildland fire will be used to protect, maintain, and enhance resources and, as nearly as possible, be allowed to function in its natural ecological role. Use of fire will be based on L/RMP and associated Fire Management Plans and will follow specific prescriptions contained in operational plans.	
Use planned and unplanned ignitions to achieve land and resource management goals. Fire management is one tool in the restoration process and should be integrated with other land management activities. Preference will be given for natural ignitions to be managed in meeting the role of fire as an ecological process. Decision support process encourages	Incident objectives will identify resource objectives for wildfires managed to achieve resource objectives. Beneficial accomplishments will be measured through specific quantified objectives.

Policy Statement	
Management Intent	Implementation Actions
strategies to manage fire to restore and maintain the natural fire regime where safe and possible.	
5 Rehabilitation and Restoration Rehabilitation and restoration efforts will be undertaken to protect and sustain ecosystems, public health and safety, and to help communities protect infrastructure.	
Conduct emergency stabilization of burned areas such that no further harm is done. Probability of success will be evaluated for rehabilitation and restoration efforts.	Burned areas will be assessed to determine suitable and effective emergency stabilization and rehabilitation needs to meet current and anticipated environmental conditions. Rehabilitation and restoration activities will be evaluated to assess effectiveness of treatments.
6 Protection Priorities The protection of human life is the single, overriding priority. Setting priorities among protecting human communities and community infrastructure, other property and improvements, and natural and cultural resources will be done based on the values to be protected, human health and safety, and the costs of protection. Once people have been committed to an incident, these human resources become the highest value to be protected.	
Resources are allocated nationally, geographically, and locally based on protection priorities. Protection of human life overrides all other priorities should response capability limits be reached. Local protection priorities are established in the L/RMP and/or FMP.	NMAC establishes national protection priorities considering maintenance of initial attack capability; protection of communities, infrastructure, property, cultural and natural resources; costs; local agency objectives; and national response framework and tasking. Geographic and local area coordination groups will establish a process to set protection priorities. The Agency Administrator will convey protection priorities, based on the L/RMP and FMP, to the geographic and national groups through an incident status report and ensure that protection

Table 1. (Continued)

Policy Statement	
Management Intent	Implementation Actions
	priorities are known and carried out by the incident commander(s).
7 Wildland Urban Interface The operational roles of federal agencies as partners in the Wildland Urban Interface are wildland firefighting, hazard fuels reduction, cooperative prevention and education, and technical assistance. Structural fire suppression is the responsibility of tribal, state, or local governments. Federal agencies may assist with exterior structural protection activities under formal Fire Protection Agreements that specify the mutual responsibilities of the partners, including funding. (Some federal agencies have structural protection authority for their facilities on lands they administer and may also enter into formal agreements to assist state and local governments with structural protection).	
Prevent the movement of wildfires from the wildlands into the WUI area, out of the WUI area into the wildlands, and improve efficiency of wildfire suppression in WUI situations. The primary responsibility for protecting private property and rural communities lies with individual property owners and local governments. Recognize that many states have wildland fire responsibility while rural fire districts have structural responsibility.	Agreements will be developed to clarify jurisdictional inter-relationships and define roles and responsibilities among local, state, tribal, and federal fire protection entities, based on each organization's enabling protection authorities and assistance/mutual aid responsibilities. Agencies will support the development and implementation of Community Wildfire Protection Plans (CWPP). The Federal wildland agencies will collaborate with tribal, state and local fire management organizations to identify and reconcile gaps in protection responsibility.
8 Planning Every area with burnable vegetation must have an approved Fire Management Plan. Fire Management Plans are strategic plans that define a program to manage wildland fires based on the area's approved land management plan. Fire Management Plans must provide for firefighter and public safety; include fire management strategies, tactics, and alternatives; address values to be protected and public health issues; and be consistent with resource management objectives, activities of the area, and environmental laws and regulations.	

Policy Statement	
Management Intent	Implementation Actions
Promote interagency and inter-governmental planning. Encourage landscape scale planning across jurisdictional boundaries.	The FMP should be interagency or intergovernmental in scope and developed on a landscape scale, where practical to take advantage of efficiency, reduce conflict and provide understanding and cooperation. L/RMP and/or FMPs will address the location and conditions under which resource benefits and protection objectives can be met.
9 Science Fire Management Plans and programs will be based on a foundation of sound science. Research will support ongoing efforts to increase our scientific knowledge of biological, physical, and sociological factors. Information needed to support fire management will be developed through an integrated interagency fire science program. Scientific results must be made available to managers in a timely manner and must be used in the development of land management plans, Fire Management Plans, and implementation plans.	
Increase the body of scientific knowledge and understanding about fire management programs through the development of management tools and transfer of knowledge to practitioners and decision makers. Social sciences are a part of the research need.	Agencies will integrate science in planning and monitoring processes. Agencies will coordinate fire-related research to improve fire management program capability. Agencies will emphasize applied science including fire and fuels, physics, social science, and operations research areas. Agencies will seek to improve decision support tools through updated data sets and advances in technology.
10 Preparedness Agencies will ensure their capability to provide safe, cost-effective fire management programs in support of land and resource management plans through appropriate planning, staffing, training, equipment, and management oversight.	

Table 1. (Continued)

Policy Statement	
Management Intent	Implementation Actions
Recognize that particular budget processes and external influences will affect capability and capacity. Size the organization to meet realistic and sustainable management objectives by effective preparedness planning on an interagency basis. Realize efficiencies by incorporating other federal, tribal, state, and local agencies and nongovernmental organizations to meet peak demands for resources. Preseason agreements are an integral part of preparedness.	Agencies will identify and realign organizational staffing and equipment mixes to implement a safe and cost effective fire management program that meets the fire management guidance identified in the L/RMP. Agencies will develop a common process for determining budget needs and cost sharing for all aspects of fire management operations. Implement training program to meet staffing levels (qualification requirements) with the emphasis on managing fires for both protection and resource management objectives. Agencies will develop agreements to efficiently utilize other federal, state, local, and non governmental resources.
11 Suppression Wildland fires are suppressed at minimum cost, considering firefighter and public safety, benefits, and values to be protected, consistent with resource objectives.	
Suppression considerations will be addressed in L/RMP and FMP's. Notwithstanding protection of life, the cost of suppression, emergency stabilization and rehabilitation must be commensurate with values to be protected.	Use a decision support process to assess conditions, analyze risk and document decisions. Predictive services products will be used to support pre-positioning resources. Agencies will coordinate staffing levels through common trend analysis of environmental indicators
12 Prevention Agencies will work together and with their partners and other affected groups and individuals to prevent unauthorized ignition of wildfires.	
Prevention focuses on the activities needed to reduce human-caused ignitions.	Agencies will work with all partners to develop and implement risk assessment, prevention, and mitigation plans to

Policy Statement	
Management Intent	Implementation Actions
Prevention includes mitigating risks and loss to ecosystems and communities.	reduce the frequency of wildfires due to human–caused ignitions..
13 Standardization Agencies will use compatible planning processes, funding mechanisms, training and qualification requirements, operational procedures, values-to-be- protected methodologies, and public education programs for all fire management activities.	
All processes are compatible and transparent so that individuals from cooperating agencies (federal, tribal, state, and local) can more effectively work together. Enhance public and cooperator understanding of wildland fire management processes.	To the extent possible, agencies will use common standards in all aspects of fire management programs so that planning and budgeting methodologies applied in one situation will provide the same results in similar circumstances. Agencies will develop and implement common operational field guidance and operational procedures to deal with all aspects of fire management operations. Agencies will streamline interagency transfer of funds to reduce fiscal inconsistencies.
14 Interagency Cooperation and Coordination Fire management planning, preparedness, prevention, suppression, fire use, restoration and rehabilitation, monitoring, research, and education will be conducted on an interagency basis with the involvement of cooperators and partners.	
Involve all participating agencies, federal, tribal, state, local, and non-governmental organizations in fire management activities. Get everyone working in concert, rather than in opposition to each other.	Ensure that fire management program actions are implemented in collaboration with cooperators and affected partners with due consideration of all management objectives. Agencies will engage cooperators and affected partners at the strategic, and program planning levels, as well as the tactical, program implementation level.
15 Communication and Education Agencies will enhance knowledge and understanding of wildland fire management policies and practices through internal and external communication and education programs. These programs will be continuously improved through the timely and effective exchange of information among all affected agencies and	

Table 1. (Continued)

Policy Statement	
Management Intent	Implementation Actions
organizations.	
Knowledge and understanding reach all personnel in the field, across agencies. Develop and provide consistent communication, education and outreach with shared messages for the public and internal staff. Have a public that understands the risk, benefits and complexity of wildland fire management.	Develop a consistent and uniform message using common terminology on importance and role of wildland fire in natural resource management. Develop understanding with the public on what we're trying accomplish with fire management. Build understanding with the public on their role when living and recreating in fire prone ecosystems.
16. Agency Administrator and Employee Roles Agency administrators will ensure that their employees are trained, certified, and made available to participate in the wildland fire program locally, regionally, and nationally as the situation demands. Employees with operational, administrative, or other skills will support the wildland fire program as necessary. Agency administrators are responsible and will be held accountable for making employees available.	
Employees participate in wildland fire operations to obtain understanding, expand capabilities, and increase organizational capacity. Assure that we maximize use of the local workforce for efficiencies of knowledge, cost and involvement. Maintain a competent and capable workforce to implement the wildland fire management program to include fuels, aviation, suppression, planning, monitoring, research, communication, finance, etc.	Agency administrators will train, qualify, and certify available personnel for local fire needs and interagency fire management priorities. Agencies will consider adjustment of annual performance expectations based on employee and program contribution to the fire effort.
17 Evaluation Agencies will develop and implement a systematic method of evaluation to determine effectiveness of projects through implementation of the 2001 Federal Fire Policy. The evaluation will assure accountability, facilitate resolution of areas of conflict, and identify resource shortages and agency priorities.	

Policy Statement	
Management Intent	Implementation Actions
Use adaptive management process to evaluate and improve the fire management program at all levels. Provide a formal review process to monitor and evaluate performance, suggest revisions, and make necessary adaptations to the implementation guidance at all organizational levels on a regular basis.	Conduct interagency, internal and periodic reviews of the fire management program (all agencies) to determine: 1) consistency of policy implementation; 2) effectiveness of interagency coordination; 3) progress towards ecosystem sustainability; 4) cost management; 5) safety.

APPENDICES

Appendix A: Glossary

The hierarchy of terminology will be those defined in law, those defined in policy, those defined in this guidance and then all other agency and interagency documentation. The NWCG Glossary of Wildland Fire Terminology will be maintained as the source of record.

Controlled burn – synonymous with Prescribed Fire.

Escaped Prescribed Fire – a prescribed fire that has exceeded or is expected to exceed prescription parameters or otherwise meets the criteria for conversion to wildfire. Criteria is specified in "Interagency Prescribed Fire – Planning and Implementation Procedures Reference Guide".

Fire Management Plan (FMP) – a plan that identifies and integrates all wildland fire management and related activities within the context of approved land/resource management plans. It defines a program to manage wildland fires (wildfire and prescribed fire). The plan is supplemented by operational plans, including but not limited to preparedness plans, preplanned dispatch plans, prescribed fire burn plans and prevention plans. Fire Management Plan's assure that wildland fire management goals and components are coordinated.

Initial Action – the actions taken by the first resources to arrive at a wildfire.

Land/Resource Management Plan (L/RMP) – a document prepared with public participation and approved by an agency administrator that provides general guidance and direction for land and resource management activities for an administrative area. The L/RMP identifies the need for fire's role in a particular area and for a specific benefit. The objectives in the L/RMP provide the basis for the development of fire management objectives and the fire management program in the designated area.

Planned Ignition –the intentional initiation of a wildland fire by hand-held, mechanical or aerial device where the distance and timing between ignition lines or points and the sequence of igniting them is determined by environmental conditions (weather, fuel, topography), firing technique, and other factors which influence fire behavior and fire effects (see prescribed fire).

Prescribed Fire—is a wildland fire originating from a planned ignition to meet specific objectives identified in a written, approved, prescribed fire plan for which NEPA requirements (where applicable) have been met prior to ignition (see planned ignition).

Protection - the actions taken to limit the adverse environmental, social, political, and economical effects of fire (FEC Briefing Paper, 3/14/2008).

Response to wildland fire - the mobilization of the necessary services and responders to a fire based on ecological, social, and legal consequences, the circumstances under which a fire occurs, and the likely consequences on firefighter and public safety and welfare, natural and cultural resources, and values to be protected.

Suppression - all the work of extinguishing a fire or confining fire spread.

Unplanned Ignition – the initiation of a wildland fire by lightning, volcanoes, unauthorized and accidental human-caused fires (see wildfire).

Use of Wildland Fire - management of either wildfire or prescribed fire to meet resource objectives specified in Land/Resource Management Plans.

Wildfire – unplanned ignition of a wildland fire (such as a fire caused by lightning, volcanoes, unauthorized and accidental human-caused fires) and escaped prescribed fires. (See unplanned ignition and escaped prescribed fire).

Wildland Fire – a general term describing any non-structure fire that occurs in the wildland.

Wildland Urban Interface (WUI) – The line, area, or zone where structures and other human development meet or intermingle with undeveloped wildland or vegetation fuels.

Appendix B: Wildland Fire Flowchart

This chart depicts, in general, the process to be taken given an ignition, regardless of source. Management actions depend on the provisions in the approved Land, Resource and Fire Management Plan and/or Fire Management Plan for an area. This chart is generally applicable to most agencies' fire management programs. However, specific exceptions may exist.

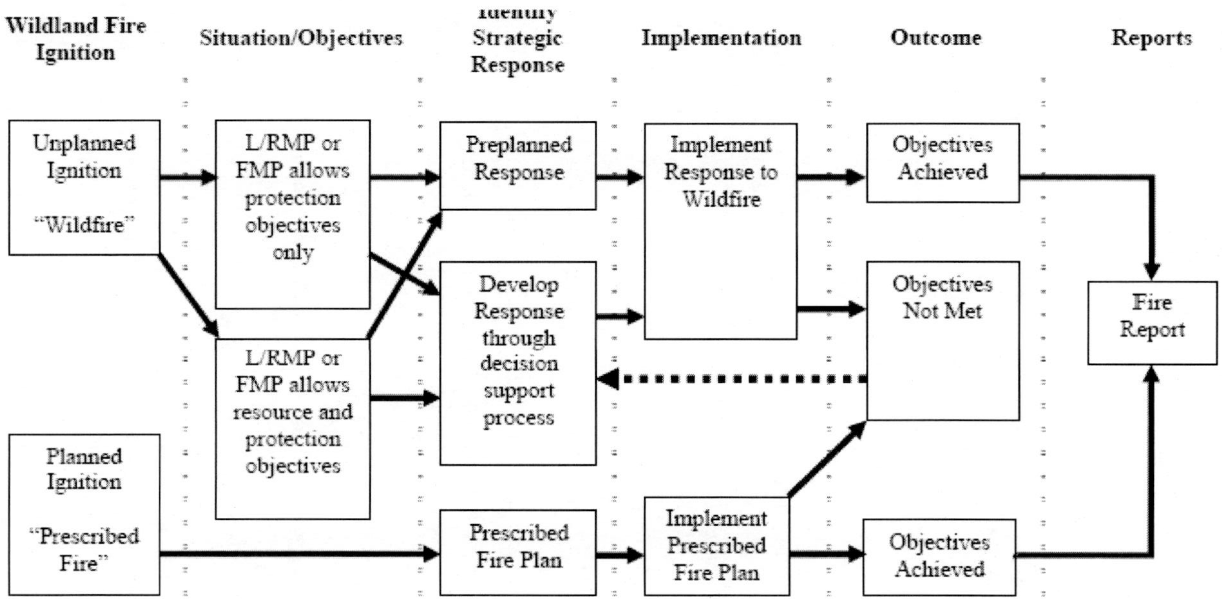

Appendix C: What Changed 2004 to 2009

The following provide some of the significant modifications that were made to the guidance in the "Interagency Strategy for the Implementation of Federal Wildland Fire Management Policy (2004)" in drafting the "Guidance for Implementation of Federal Wildland Fire Management Policy (2009)." To simplify the discussion the "Interagency Strategy for the Implementation of Federal Wildland Fire Management Policy (2004)" will be referred to as "Strategy" and the "Guidance for Implementation of Federal Wildland Fire Management Policy (2009)" will be referred to as "Guidance".

Strategy: Provided seven operational clarification statements.

Guidance: Provides nine statements of guidance for implementation.

Strategy: Operational Clarification statement 1) "Only one management objective will be applied to a wildland fire. Wildland fires will either be managed for resource benefits or suppressed. A wildland fire cannot be managed for both objectives concurrently. If two wildland fires converge, they will be managed as a single wildland fire."

Guidance: "A wildland fire may be concurrently managed for one or more objectives and objectives can change as the fire spreads across the landscape. Objectives are affected by changes in fuels, weather, topography; varying social understanding and tolerance; and involvement of other governmental jurisdictions having different missions and objectives."

Strategy: Operational Clarification statement 2) "Human caused wildland fires will be suppressed in every instance and will not be managed for resource benefits.

Guidance: "Initial action on human-caused wildfire will be to suppress the fire at the lowest cost with the fewest negative consequences with respect to firefighter and public safety."

Strategy: Operational Clarification statement 3) "Once a wildland fire has been managed for suppression objectives, it may never be managed for resource benefit objectives."

Guidance: "A wildland fire may be concurrently managed for one or more objectives and objectives can change as the fire spreads across the landscape. Objectives are affected by changes in fuels, weather, topography; varying social understanding and tolerance; and involvement of other governmental jurisdictions having different missions and objectives."

Strategy: Operational Clarification statement 4) "The Appropriate Management Response (AMR) is any specific action suitable to meet Fire Management Unit (FMU) objectives. Typically, the AMR ranges across a spectrum of tactical options (from monitoring to intensive management actions). The AMR is developed by using FMU strategies and objectives identified in the Fire Management Plan."

Guidance: The term Appropriate Management Response is removed from implementation guidance with "Response to Wildland Fire" as the policy area defining the actions for managing a wildland fire.

Strategy: Operational Clarification statement 5) "The Wildland Fire Situation Analysis process is used to determine and document the suppression strategy from the full range of responses available for suppression operations. Suppression strategies are designed to meet the policy objectives of suppression."

Guidance: "Managers will use a decision support process to guide and document wildfire management decisions. The process will provide situational assessment, analyze hazards and risk, define implementation actions, and document decisions and rationale for those decisions.

Strategy: Operational Clarification statement 6) "Wildland fire use is the result of a natural event. The Land/Resource Management Plan, or the Fire Management Plan, will identify areas where the strategy of wildland fire use is suitable. The Wildland Fire Implementation Plan (WFIP) is the tool that examines the available response strategies to determine if a fire is being considered for wildland fire use."

Guidance: "Managers will use a decision support process to guide and document wildfire management decisions. The process will provide situational assessment, analyze hazards and risk, define implementation actions, and document decisions and rationale for those decisions."

Strategy: Operational Clarification statement 7) "When a prescribed fire or a fire designated for wildland fire use is no longer achieving the intended resource management objectives and contingency or mitigation actions have failed, the fire will be declared a wildfire. Once a wildfire, it cannot be returned to a prescribed fire or wildland fire use status."

Guidance: "Managers will use a decision support process to guide and document wildfire management decisions. The process will provide situational assessment, analyze hazards and risk, define implementation actions, and document decisions and rationale for those decisions."

Strategy: Policy Implementation Flowchart.

Guidance: Updated Appendix F: Wildland Fire Flowchart from Review and Update of the 1995 Federal Wildland Fire Management Policy (2001) to reflect implementation terminology of planned and unplanned ignitions. (See Appendix B).

INDEX

D

E

F

G

H

I

J

L

M

N

O

P

R

S